Learner Services

CITY COLLEGE
NORWICH

KT-471-554

stamped below

2 7 MAY 2010

2 7 NOV 2015

A FINE WILL BE CHARGED FOR OVERDUE ITEMS

Karen Castle

NORWICH CITY COLLEGE

Stock No.	234 237	
Class	370·7 CAS	
Cat.	SSA	Proc	3WL

www.learningmatters.co.uk

234   237

First published in 2010 by Learning Matters Ltd.

All rights reserved. No part of this publication may be reproduced, stored in a retrieval system, or transmitted in any form or by any means, electronic, mechanical, photocopying, recording, or otherwise, without prior permission in writing from Learning Matters.

© 2010 Karen Castle

British Library Cataloguing in Publication Data
A CIP record for this book is available from the British Library.

ISBN 978 1 84445 287 3

The right of Karen Castle to be identified as the Author of this Work has been asserted by her in accordance with Copyright, Design and Patents Act 1988.

Cover design by Topics
Text design by Phil Barker
Project management by Deer Park Productions, Tavistock, Devon
Typeset by PDQ Typesetting Ltd, Newcastle-under-Lyme, Staffordshire
Printed and bound in Great Britain by Bell & Bain Ltd, Glasgow

Learning Matters Ltd
33 Southernhay East
Exeter EX1 1NX
Tel: 01392 215560
info@learningmatters.co.uk
www.learningmatters.co.uk

Contents

The author

Karen Castle

Karen Castle is Head of Academic Quality at the Institute of Education, Manchester Metropolitan University. Working on academic quality and enhancement across the Institute, Karen is also involved in the development of the MTL course.

Introduction

This book has been designed to offer practical support to teachers embarking on master's-level study. In particular it is geared towards people taking part in teacher training programmes that lead to the Master's in Teaching and Learning (MTL).

The current government, at time of writing, has been clear in its agenda that all teachers will be trained to master's level (DCSF, 2008). Organisations responsible for initial teacher training (ITT) are required to ensure that programmes leading to qualified teacher status (QTS) are delivered and assessed at the appropriate level. From January 2010 in the North West of England, and all National Challenge schools, NQTs will be offered the opportunity to complete a Masters in Teaching and Learning.

This book will also be useful to teachers who are already qualified and working towards master's degrees as part of their continuing professional development (CPD). These teachers will not have been exposed to master's-level study when they first trained, and therefore, this study skills guide will offer tips and advice to support their CPD. I have identified, through research recently carried out as part of a doctorate thesis, that many teachers are not familiar with master's-level study skills, in particular such issues as portfolio development and reflective critical analysis. This book is designed to demystify some of these areas and to encourage teachers to read more specialist and focused texts on topics and themes that they feel should be further developed.

The way in which teachers have viewed themselves within the professional arena would appear to have changed over time. In the early twentieth century, many teachers felt that they were professionally inferior if they did not have any certificated qualification (Gardner, 1995). Later in the same century, teachers ceased comparing themselves professionally with the medical and legal professions, opting instead to compare the teaching profession with police and other public-sector workers (Lawn and Grace, 1987). This would still seem to be the case today. News reports and similar media coverage usually compare teaching with other public-sector organisations such as nursing and policing. Kydd (1997, p116) reported that the *traditional notions of teacher professionalism* have been restructured, in terms of teachers being managers of school systems and policies as opposed to curriculum. McKenzie (2001) has argued that changes to the teaching profession have been so profound since the 1940s that teaching has experienced a loss of status and influence that has resulted in a loss of security. She further suggests that this has led to the question of whether it remains appropriate to use the term 'professional'. This view was seemingly considered by the government, as at the end of the twentieth century, the White Paper *Excellence in schools* was published (DfEE, 1997) in which the issues of teacher demoralisation and perceived low status were addressed. The government also introduced the General

Teaching Council (GTC), and charged the council with raising the status of the teaching profession. Contrastingly, there emerged a school of thought that suspected that the government of the mid-1990s was intent on the 'deprofessionalisation' of teaching, by ensuring teacher training focused on subject and craft skills rather than professional issues, and by the support of the National Curriculum, which many considered removed autonomy from teachers (Whitty, 1997).

Education in the twenty-first century in the United Kingdom is driven largely by policy and focused on outcomes which could, albeit in part, have resulted in teachers' identities being in flux (Stronach et al., 2002). It is this point that is of particular interest, and which was key to the development of this book, as the way in which teachers identify themselves could impact on the way in which they approach their own professional status and ultimately, their practice development.

It could be argued that, in order to develop and/or maintain any degree of professional identity within the community of practice that is the school, teachers need to be trained and qualified to an appropriate standard that offers a parity nationally. Similarly, teaching as a profession should explore the opportunities to develop both collegially and in terms of acquiring knowledge and skills. In respect of modern teaching for example, the ways in which local and national policy impact upon their organisations, the construction of educational discourse, the limitations and benefits of political agenda and the significance of research and innovation will all impact on the professional discourse that is teaching. This notion is given further credence in particular with reference to the argument by Smyth (1995, p217) that teachers as an occupational group have *failed to keep up with the pace of social and economic change*. Smyth further found that education and school reforms during the last two decades have led to teachers feeling jaded and betrayed in terms of their professional status and position within the school.

Many of these negative feelings and perceptions from and about teachers will be given the opportunity of being challenged by the introduction of the MTL. At least, this is what the government would like to see, and it is what many educational specialists would also advocate. The fundamental issue for the introduction of the MTL will be the question of how it is received by the teachers themselves, both those groups of teachers who will be embarking on it as part of the ITT programmes, and also the existing teachers who will be witnessing these changes taking place to their professional training which they may not be able to relate to, nor understand.

Political discourses will impact on institutions and organisations, to varying degrees, and with this in mind and with respect to the relationship between teachers' training and CPD and the organisation, Oldroyd and Hall (1997) argued that teacher development and school improvement are inextricably linked. However, Forde et al. (2006) warn that wider socio-economic factors also contribute to the effectiveness of schools, and further to this, Campbell et al. (2004) suggested that there would seem to be tensions between the teachers' development needs, and the needs of the organisation. They suggest that it is merely an 'assumption' that better developed and qualified teachers result in high-achieving pupils; this is in further contrast to Blandford (2000), who assumes that well-developed teachers lead to improvements within the classroom. That the development of teachers leads to well-qualified pupils is not for debate here; however, the current government clearly believes that well trained and qualified teachers have a positive impact on what is learnt within the classroom, and this has significant implications for teachers' training, their CPD and the level at which it is offered.

If we consider the Green Paper, *Learning and Teaching: A strategy for professional development* (DfES, 2001), it would seem that the current government wants to rekindle the notion of schools becoming learning communities. Most of the MTL will be work-based, teachers will be given access to mentors, coaches and tutors; however, a large part of the MTL is focused on teachers reflecting on their own practice area. This style of learning is something of a move away from the traditional, university-based ITT that has previously been delivered. Universities will retain a fundamental and critical role in teacher training and in particular, the MTL; however, there will be changes to this role and the way in which it is acted out. Universities will also be charged with providing CPD opportunities for existing teachers at master's level. Many have already entered into partnerships with schools and local authorities (LAs) for this purpose. The main changes relating to CPD are demonstrated in the document *Learning and Teaching: A strategy for professional development* (DfES, 2001) in which is detailed the government's focus for the way in which teachers' CPD will evolve. The following points offer a framework against which teachers can interpret how their CPD will be developed over the coming years.

- Implementing the CPD framework strategy will require sustained commitment and partnership between government, its agencies, General Teaching Council (GTC), teachers, heads, schools, local authorities and higher education institutions (HEIs).
- Head teachers will be made more accountable for the quality of professional development in their schools, they will be encouraged to raise the profile of CPD for teachers for whom it is a low priority.
- Funding will be increased to enable schools to become 'learning communities' and in particular with regard to extending 'best practice research' and 'teacher international professional development'.
- Organisations such as local authorities and higher education institutions will have a key role to play in providing focused and practical development opportunities, and where possible, enable the CPD activities to be fully accredited.
- Teachers will need to take responsibility for their own professional development.

(DfES, 2001)

The government has identified that schools will become effective learning communities, where the:

> *Vision and commitment of the head teacher, supported by the senior management team and placing the professional development of their staff, is at the heart of their approach to school improvement.*

(DfES, 2001)

Much of what is written in this book has been developed from my experience of working with, and ethnographically researching teachers, both those who are new to the profession and taking part in ITT programmes, and also teachers who have been taking part in CPD activities.

In order to achieve the accolade of being able to 'master' a particular area of education, teachers will need to demonstrate that they can successfully complete a set of accredited modules that make up the three phases of the MTL or other master's degrees. In order to do this, many teachers will need to develop higher-level study skills. They will need to be guided and supported in an effective and sensitive manner towards this level of study. A common misconception of teachers is that they already possess these higher-level study skills. However, it is evident that this in some cases, is not true, and teachers are often made to feel inadequate if they don't somehow immediately, and without further training, demonstrate a high academic prowess.

This study skills guide assumes that teachers do possess a high standard of academic practice; however, it does not expect teachers to be able to relate to master's-level study at the outset, but rather, on completion of the text, it is expected that teachers would begin to feel confident with, and develop the skills necessary to be comfortable with, study and practice at this level. This book has been designed as a practical support to teachers who are embarking on master's-level CPD; it is intended that teachers will use this publication as a handbook or guidebook to support their studies, referring to the book as a reference throughout their training.

Chapter 1 focuses on learning styles and offers teachers the opportunity to reflect on their preferred learning style. It also looks at theories and models of learning, and suggests how theory can underpin and focus the practice of learning. This chapter primarily serves to familiarise teachers with some of the different theories of learning and allows them to identify how a model could be something that can be adapted and adopted for use in the practice area. At the end of the chapter the teacher is encouraged to reflect areas of their own practice in terms of theoretical influence.

Chapter 2 looks at how the individual teacher can identify the study skills they already possess, and build on these at an appropriate level. It addresses areas such as motivation, time management and long- and short-term targets. This chapter will also offer suggestions to ways of studying from and getting the most out of different scenarios, for example, attending a lecture, reading, discussions, problem-solving and practical activities such as role play, case studies and presentations.

Chapter 3 addresses the skills needed in order to design and develop an essay that is at the level appropriate to the MTL. These study skills include the development of academic writing skills, for example, planning and structuring an essay and developing an argument, referencing and critically analysing the literature around the area being studied.

Chapter 4 introduces the teacher to the area of research. In particular, it will identify different research approaches and address the overall aims of research. It will provide the opportunity for the teacher to identify areas within their own practice that could support a research project.

Chapter 5 will look at the area of research in more depth, and in so doing will address the subject of research methodology. The chapter will discuss action research, case study research and ethnography and will identify the role played by insider and outsider researchers. It will also identify different techniques for managing and interpreting data and will suggest ways of disseminating the findings.

Chapter 6 addresses the areas of critique and analysis, and in so doing, offers the opportunity for teachers to begin to develop these skills from the perspective of classroom researchers. It will encourage teachers to develop an argument, in terms of analysing the multidimensional perspectives of school-based situations with which they are faced and which, in many cases, need to manage.

Chapter 7 addresses methods of assessing the modules undertaken on the MTL. It will discuss and analyse the methods of developing a portfolio, writing an essay and preparing and producing a presentation.

Chapter 8 looks at the future of teachers' CPD. It will discuss the findings from research and address areas such as lifelong learning and workplace learning. It will demonstrate the practicalities of studying in the twenty-first century, in particular using information technology and looking at how schools can become learning communities.

Case studies

Throughout this book, each chapter will offer case studies as a way in which you can examine a real situation and learn from the different aspects and perspectives of each of the case studies. Case studies have been included in order that you can begin to develop reflection and interpretation skills from real situations appertaining to teachers' training and CPD.

The first case study in this introduction addresses the perspective of a teacher who has actively engaged in master's-level CPD and the second, from the perspective of a teacher who has disengaged from master's-level CPD. Read through the two case studies and examine the different facets of each in order that you can weigh up the different perspectives. What questions would you put to each of the teachers if you had the opportunity? Why do you want to know this information in particular? What are your feelings with regard to the views of each of the teachers? Each situation will have positive and negative connotations; you should identify what these are and compare these to your own feelings and values.

Case Study 1

The teacher in this case study has been teaching for two years, she is 28 years old, married without children and regards CPD as a contractual obligation, and *as much part of the job as teaching in the classroom*. She has a particular interest in the integration of foreign pupils and has the full support of the head teacher for her CPD. This teacher has been informed that the data from the research project she has begun will feed into the organisation's policy for the integration of foreign pupils, and furthermore, has obtained

HEI accreditation for the project, which would result in her receiving 40 master's-level credits for the successful completion of the research study. She also indicated that she would write a paper following this research investigation, either for a journal or for a conference. Many of her teaching colleagues have not been as supportive as the head teacher, suggesting that she is *wasting her time, trying to find out the impossible,* and spending time on something that will make no difference to anything in the end. She has attended 85 per cent of the HEI study sessions and 100 per cent of tutorials. She has maintained good communication links via email and telephone with the tutor and submitted draft work as requested. She is determined to complete the appropriate amount of CPD modules that would enable her to achieve a master's degree. The reason she gave for this was to *keep up with newly qualified teachers* (NQTs) and to enable her to have opportunity for promotion in the future.

Case Study 2

The teacher featured in this case study is in her late forties, married with grown-up children and has been teaching for 18 years. She indicated that she was *pushed* into registering for CPD by the current trend within school to carry out some sort of development. She felt that she had been an effective teacher for *many years* and had *never had a bad annual report,* therefore she did not feel the necessity to engage in any CPD. Due to an *increase in impetus on behalf of the head teacher* to *drum up* as many teachers as possible to take part CPD, she felt coerced into *signing up for the accredited CPD that the other staff were doing.* After about three weeks, she began to *fall back* with the CPD work and stopped attending the university sessions. She was late submitting work and had two essays returned as they were not of an appropriate standard. This led to her becoming more reluctant to continue and she reported feeling *stupid* and *thick;* she went on to say that: *the trouble is that the university and the local authority think all teachers are academics, and they are not, if they want to make us into academics, then they need to give us time, support, funding and patience.* She withdrew from the course that she had started and, furthermore, reported that she was *very reluctant* to embark on any future CPD.

Reflective Task

Take some time to think about your own training and any schools within which you have been placed. What do you feel about the government agenda for teaching to become a master's-level profession? What do you feel are the advantages of this, and what are the limitations? Given that the change to training will eventually impact on existing teachers and their CPD, try to identify what type of CPD is being carried out within the schools in which you have worked. Is it accredited at master's level? Are teachers engaged in school-based

CPD or are they participating in CPD outside of the organisation? How does the head teacher support CPD? What is your own view of the CPD that is being carried out? What projects are taking place within the school or within individual classrooms? Could these be used as CPD activities?

Practical Tasks

Log on to the government web sites: **www.dfes.gov.uk**
www.dscf.gov.uk
www.tda.gov.uk

Have a look at the way in which each of them promotes teachers' training and CPD. Identify in more detail, how the government views ITT and CPD and consider the implications for this in the practice area.

Discuss your findings with colleagues at school, and in so doing, attempt to discover their views in terms of how they value the change to ITT and CPD.

Summary

The current government, at time of writing, has identified its agenda in terms of teachers' ITT and CPD and, in so doing, has outlined the priority to develop teaching as a master's-level profession. This has implications for the way in which local authorities and universities work with schools in order to secure funding, accreditation and appropriate academic support for teachers taking part in ITT and CPD. It would seem that, in the past, teachers perceived themselves as professionals in a manner that is considerably different to that of teachers today. Historically, they compared themselves with medical and legal professionals; however, in recent times, the comparison has been drawn to public-sector professionals. There seems to be a connection between professional status and training and this could have some significance on the way in which teachers approach their practice and the way in which children learn within the classroom.

Practical study skills form the framework for this book, and teachers are encouraged to reflect and consider case studies throughout.

References and **Further reading**
Blandford, S. (2000) *Managing Professional Development in Schools*. Abingdon: Routledge.

Brown, P. and Lauder, H. (1997) Education, globalization and economic development, in Halsey, A., Lauder, H., Brown, P. and Wells, A. (eds) *Education: Culture economy society*. Oxford: Oxford University Press.

Campbell, A., McNamara, O. and Gilroy, P. (2004) *Practitioner Research and Professional Development in education*. London: Paul Chapman Publishing.

Day, C. (1999) *Developing Teachers: The challenges of lifelong learning*. Abingdon: Falmer Press.

DCSF (2008) *Being the Best for Our Children: Releasing talent for teaching and learning*. London: DCSF.

DfES (1997) *Excellence in Schools*. White Paper. London: HMSO.

DfES (1998) *Teachers Meeting the Challenge of Change*. Green Paper. London: HMSO.

DfES (2001) *Learning and Teaching: A strategy for professional development*. Green Paper. London: HMSO.

DfES (2005) *Higher Standards: Better schools for all*. White Paper. London: DfES.

Forde, C., McMahon, M., McPhee, A. and Patrick, F. (2006) *Professional Development, Reflection and Enquiry*. London: Paul Chapman Publishing.

Gardner, P. (1995) Teacher training and changing professional identity in early 20th century England. *Journal of Education for Teaching*, 21 (2): 191–217.

Kydd, L. (1997) Teacher professionalism and managerialism, in Kydd, L., Crawford, M. and Riches, C. (eds) *Professional Development for Educational Management*. Buckingham: Open University Press.

Lawn, M. and Grace, G (1987) *Teachers: The culture and politics of work*. Abingdon. Falmer

Mahony, P. and Hextall, I. (2000) *Reconstructing Teaching: Standards, performance and accountability*. Abingdon: RoultedgeFalmer.

McKenzie, J. (2001) *Changing Education*. London: Prentice Hall.

Oldroyd, D. and Hall, V. (1997) Identifying needs and priorities in professional development, in Kydd, L., Crawford, M. and Riches, C. (eds) *Professional Development for Educational Management*. Buckingham: Open University Press.

Price Waterhouse Coopers (2001) *Teacher Workload Survey*. Final Report. London: DfES.

Smyth, J. (1995) *Critical Discourses on Teacher Development*. London: Cassell.

Stenhouse, L. (1975) *An Introduction to Curriculum Research and Development*. London: Heinemann Educational.

Stronach, I., Corbin, B., McNamara, O., Stark, S. and Warne, T (2002) Towards an uncertain politics of professionalism: Teacher and nurse identities in flux. *Journal of Educational policy*, 17 (1): 109–38.

Training and Development Agency (2005) *Continuing Professional Development: National priorities for teachers*. Circular Annex B, on **www.tda.org.uk**

Whitty, G. (1997) Marketization, the state and the re-formation of the teaching profession, in Halsey, A., Lauder, H., Brown, P. and Wells, A. (eds) *Education: Culture economy society*. Oxford: Oxford Press.

CHAPTER 1

Theories, models and learning styles

By the end of this chapter, you will be able to identify:
• different models and theories of learning;
• different learning styles;
• how theory can be used to underpin practice;
• how you can use models to support your own practice.

Links to standards
This chapter will help you to address the following professional teaching standards.

C2 Hold positive values and attitudes and adopt high standards of behaviour in your professional role.

C3 Maintain an up-to-date knowledge and understanding of the professional duties of teachers and the statutory framework within which they work, and contribute to the development, implementation and evaluation of the policies and practice of your workplace, including those designed to promote equality of opportunity.

C7 Evaluate your performance and be committed to improving your practice through appropriate professional development.

C10 Have a good up-to-date working knowledge and understanding of a range of teaching, learning and behaviour management strategies and know how to use and adapt them, including how to personalise learning to provide opportunities for all learners to achieve their potential.

P2 Have an extensive knowledge and understanding of how to use and adapt a range of teaching, learning and behaviour management strategies, including how to personalise learning to provide opportunities for all learners to achieve their potential.

Introduction

This chapter addresses some of the theory and concepts that underpin the process of learning. By 'learning', I do not mean the easily forgotten unstructured and often bland information that is pummelled into the minds of individuals when being urged to conform (reminiscent of one of the old methods of teaching children multiplication), but instead, it refers to *meaningful learning, interesting learning and a state where the individual has the drive to learn*, that state which motivates the individual to get to the bottom of what is happening in a situation – the state of discovery, enlightenment and development. This chapter is concerned with the relationship of theory to the meaningful learning that takes place. One of the criticisms offered by teachers when talking about theory, is that it is often written in a terminology and language that is inaccessible and difficult to understand. Many teachers view themselves as practical people and this is sometimes seen in opposition to being theoretical. Murray and Moore (2006, p165) refer to the theory–practice divide, which suggests there is something of a chasm between the two concepts. In order to fully benefit from this handbook, teachers are advised to view theory as something that is inextricably linked to practice, something that offers explanation and support for practical activities. If teachers do not fully engage with theory, some of the fundamental principles that underpin teaching and learning will be unrecognised and redundant.

Reading through this chapter, it is advisable that you regularly reflect on your own style and practice, remaining open to experiment with new information. While working through the MTL, you will draw on your experience, knowledge and practice of being a teacher and a learner, you will identify with different theories and models and be able to demonstrate how your practice is influenced by these theories. There is no single all-embracing theory that you will be able to refer to as being *the* theory that you subscribe to, or that best supports your practice, but rather you are more likely to identify with elements of several different theories. This, albeit in part, reflects the rich diversity both of the teaching profession and the professional development arena.

This chapter addresses some of the theories and models of learning and in doing so identifies with different learning styles. It is intended to provide a jargon-free, practical and straightforward approach. It provides an opportunity for you to reflect on your practice and on your learning that takes place within the classroom, while considering and comparing with the theory or theories that underpin your practice and learning.

Bush and West Burnham (1994) identified that theory provides a rationale for decision-making. During the course of your working day you will be called upon to make many decisions, both concerning the children in your care, the organisation within which you work and relating to your development. You probably make decisions without even thinking about the concept of relating a theory to that decision. This chapter will highlight some of the theories that can underpin the decisions that you make. Senge (1990, p202) argued that learning or assimilating new information eventually leads to a change in the way you act, rather than merely taking in new information or creating new ideas. He highlighted the importance of being able to acknowledge the difference in what we say ('espoused theories') and what we do ('theories in use'). One way of personalising this is to firstly think of something that you are good at, something that you can confidently do well and then reflect on how you became good at this.

Learning styles

You will learn at a different pace and in a different manner from your colleagues and from other teachers taking part in the MTL. It is probably likely that up to now you have been more concerned with the ways in which your pupils learn and assimilate information. You will have designed and delivered lessons to take into account the manner and pace at which your pupils learn. Furthermore, you are probably most likely to be responsible for the ways in which children learn. I am now going to suggest that you take some time to reflect on your own learning and therefore, on how an adult learns.

When it comes to learning, adults differ from children in that they have their own individual expectations of their learning; these expectations have been developed as a result of life experiences and knowledge gained from these life chances which have been generated through professional and personal circumstances. Adults normally expect to be treated as adults, and therefore spoken to as adults. Your MTL tutors will not prescribe your learning, nor direct you in the sense that school teachers direct children, but rather, they will identify what you will need to learn and offer ways in which you would consider it appropriate to do so. When teaching children, it is necessary to establish some degree of discipline within the classroom in order for learning to take place; in an adult learning scenario this is not normally a priority and the tutor will be less likely to demonstrate 'crowd control' skills, but will concentrate on the subject area. Adults also have the expectation that their learning will be related to the workplace and will enhance their vocational skills. The MTL will underpin your classroom practice and will, in many cases, offer the opportunity for you to reflect on practice and make changes where necessary. You will add to your knowledge of education and be able to demonstrate new techniques and methods. It is argued that adult learners generally react against being asked to study subjects that they feel have no relevance to their work. It is also felt that adult learners normally expect to have to work quite hard when learning. This may be as a result of memories from their own schooling, it may be as a result of realising that any new knowledge needs to be worked at. Teachers in particular, tend to perceive CPD and learning as something that is time-consuming and difficult, it is often thought to be something that takes place outside of the workplace, and therefore, somehow removed and remote from the teacher's role. The mantra: *I am too busy to do any more training* can be heard in staffrooms across the country many times. University tutors appreciate that you are likely to have homes and families to care for and are already working for a significant amount of time at school and that you will have other pressures to negotiate, therefore, the work you do for the MTL will be negotiated with you and where possible, designed to fit around these other aspects of your life. It is important to consider that learning does not need to be excessively time-consuming, as you can generate learning opportunities and learning scenarios within your place of work.

Teachers and their own learning

As a teacher, you need to know what you want your pupils to learn. You identify this by means of learning outcomes. Similarly, you will have aims and objectives that you want your pupils to achieve. Your own training and CPD are the same. In order to successfully complete a training programme, you will need to achieve the aims and objectives and be able to address the learning outcomes. These are usually clearly stated on course literature at the beginning of your course. It is advisable that you spend some time really getting the grasp of what the learning outcomes are asking you to do. For example, are they asking you to 'describe' something? In which case you need to be able to understand what this means. You might be instructed to 'analyse', or 'critically analyse' something. Don't be put off by these words, find out what they mean to you and give some thought to how you might address them as learning outcomes. Critical analysis is covered later in this book and will go into more detail of how you can become a critical practitioner. Other words often used for MTL outcomes are: argue, identify, critique, appraise and reflect. I would urge you to really understand these phrases before embarking on the MTL as once you have understood them you will address your learning in a much more focused way. Chapter 6 analyses these phrases in more detail. Given that the issue we are concerned with here is the way in which you meet the learning outcome criteria, the sooner you can be confident with your understanding of what is being asked, the sooner you will be able to apply yourself to what it is you are studying. The rest of this chapter will address the theory that underpins this learning. While reading through this text you are advised to take some time to reflect on your practice and learning and in doing so identify which theory or theories most closely resemble your own methods; as mentioned earlier, it may well be that parts of several different theories underpin your own practice.

There are three main groups or domains by which people learn: psychomotor, cognitive and affective.

1. **Psychomotor** – Learning skills which involve manually using objects, tools and equipment. Psychomotor learning is learning 'to do' something, to use manual dexterity, and if we break down the word: 'psych' suggests a cognitive aspect, for example, a situation which must be remembered or understood in order to carry out the 'motor' aspect, which suggests movement or physicality. Examples include: making a display wall, typing a letter, playing the piano and using the whiteboard. According to Dave (1975), the taxonomy of learning in the psychomotor domain considers the following to be important, beginning with the least difficult.

   - Imitation: observes and tries to repeat as seen.
   - Manipulation: carries out skills following instruction rather than observation.
   - Precision: reproduces a task or skill with accuracy and precision, separate from the original source.
   - Articulation: combines one or several skills in sequence with each other.
   - Naturalisation: completes one or several skills with confidence and competence.

2. **Cognitive** – Learning skills which involve memorising information and recalling factual information and using mental activities such as perception. You can improve your cognitive learning skills by visually or verbally associating things – grouping them together, for example; hat, coat, scarf and gloves. Similarly, you learn cognitively by repetition, for example, your car registration number or your telephone number; you learn these numbers by constantly repeating them, you can do the same with facts,

multiplication tables used to be learnt by this method. The cognitive domain is also demonstrated when testing, as we ask learners to recall what they have assimilated. Using mnemonics, for example, 'i before e except after c' and 'bLue Left – bRown Right' for the way in which a plug should be wired, are useful cognitive skills to develop.

The cognitive domain has the following categories, beginning with the least difficult.

- Knowledge: recall of information.
- Comprehension: interprets and summarises information.
- Application: applies knowledge to a situation different from the original learning scenario.
- Analysis: Divides the whole situation into separate parts and identifies relationships between the parts.
- Synthesis: forms new concepts from the original situation.
- Evaluation: makes decisions and judgements based on rationale from learning.

(Bloom, 1960)

3. **Affective** – The affective domain concerns feelings, attitudes, values and emotions. In affective learning the student begins by being aware of stimuli in a passive role, for example, listening to a discussion or a lecture. An example of a higher level of affective learning would be demonstrated when the student has listened to the information, but has then taken it a step further by realising their own values and beliefs regarding the information and has accomplished a degree of learning as a result. The major categories of the affective domain are as follows.

- Receiving: The learner aware of information by listening.
- Responding: The learner reacts to stimuli, e.g. by answering questions.
- Valuing: The learner offers an attitude or belief regarding the stimuli, not necessarily agreeing with it.
- Organising: The learner commits to a set of values.
- Characterising: The learner inputs their own beliefs and values and their total behaviour becomes consistent with these newly developed values.

(Adapted from Reece and Walker, 1997)

An example of learning in the affective domain would be a situation where a student attends a workshop on a health and safety course where they are exposed to theories and techniques, where they are able to listen and consider. Following on from the workshop, the students are asked to move some boxes of paper to a store cupboard. The skills they developed from the earlier workshop are automatically applied so they lift the boxes according to the correct health and safety techniques.

Case Study

Jill is a primary school teacher, responsible for children at Key Stage 2. She has been involved recently in a school programme to link up with a school in France in order to form a 'pen friend' club for the children within her school. Jill took time in the planning and development of this project to ensure that she addressed most of the issues that would arise before they became problems. She liaised with the school teachers at the Normandy school, speaking to them on many occasions, and emailing often. She spoke to the parents of the children at her school and allayed any fears that were put forward, and she presented her project to the school governors and obtained their backing, before carrying the project forward. Jill wanted to provide a structured framework for the children to follow, so she suggested that the first contact would be to introduce themselves to their French pen friend; the second contact would be to introduce their family and the area in which they lived; following contacts would have similar topics and she was planning to visit the Normandy school in the summer.

Jill was keen to take part in CPD, but she felt that the school pen friend project would take too much of her time, on top of her already heavy workload. She therefore looked into how she could turn this project into a learning scenario for herself, and one which she could use as a focus for her own CPD. The head teacher supported Jill's project and would offer positive feedback and encouragement whenever possible.

Reflective Task

Reflecting on the above case study, try to identify which theories, or parts of theory, underpin Jill's development. Assuming that Jill had begun to develop a personal CPD file, what evidence of her development on this project could she include in her file?

Now give some thought to projects that you have been involved with in school. How did your knowledge increase as a result of this? What new skills did you learn that you could develop to use in the future? If you were asked to talk to other teachers about your development, what would you say were the positive and negative aspects of this project?

How could the behaviourist theory be interpreted in this case study?

Which theories or parts of theory can you identify with in your own learning to date?

Theories and models of learning

There is a great deal of theory regarding how we learn and there are a number of theorists who have developed concepts of learning. It is worth considering that a theory is something that has been developed from which you can either identify with, or contradict. If you think about the grand theories, for example, feminism or Marxism, you may not agree with the theory, but you would be able to identify how that theory has shaped areas of society and possibly how it has influenced you as a person and a professional, and so it is with theories of learning. If we look at feminism in a little more detail, it is evident that there are different aspects of feminism and women often relate to one aspect and not another. Ahmed et al. (2000, p1) argued that feminism *is not one set of struggles, it has mobilised different women in different times and places, who are all seeking transformations, but who are not necessarily seeking the same thing.* Rather than address all the theories of learning in detail, four of the main areas are discussed here.

Behaviourism

In the early twentieth century, it was believed that by studying the behaviour and activity of animals, human behaviour could be explained. The behaviourists used a stimulus-response model to study behaviour; for example, a dog was given food at the same time that a specific sound was made. The dog responded by salivating at the time the food was offered. After a while, the dog salivated just on hearing the sound without the food being produced. Pavlov was the behaviourist carrying out this experiment, and he called this 'conditioned learning'. The general consensus was that a stimulus is more likely to offer a certain response from the learner if similar past responses have been beneficial to the learner and have been acknowledged with praise or approval of some kind. Stimulus-response learning is also known as 'trial and error learning', which involves trying out different types of response until the appropriate one is discovered, the appropriate response being rewarded in some way. Instrumental learning attempts to identify how learners behave when they are exposed to a stimulus. In other words, the theory of behaviourism suggests that we learn by being exposed to some sort of stimulus that provokes us to respond, and providing that response is positively reinforced, we will repeat the action. Learning is brought about by the association of the response and positive reinforcement.

For example, if you produce a piece of work, maybe a couple of paragraphs from an MTL essay, and you want to get it checked out to see if what you have done is the correct style, etc., the response you get in the way of feedback from the tutor is crucial to the way in which you will complete the essay.

Neo-behaviourism

The neo-behaviourists introduced a more humanist approach to the stimulus-response theory. They felt that people respond to stimuli using their feelings, beliefs and values. The neo-behaviourists stated that learners need to receive 'reinforcement' continually throughout their learning, for example, a nod of the head from the tutor, or a positive verbal response. They felt that learning needed to be rewarded frequently, particularly in the early stages.

This type of learning has implications for distance learning, as with this method the tutor is not always present throughout to be able to give positive verbal response or offer encouraging facial expressions. The current trend in some areas to encourage 'online' learning also needs to address this. One of the main barriers to distance and online learning is the fact that there is minimal fact-to-face contact with the tutor and other members of the group.

Gestalt (insight learning)

The gestalt theory argues that the whole or overall perspective is more important than the individual elements of a scenario. For example, if we consider the MTL, the gestaltists could argue that the ultimate qualification of a master's degree is more important than the individual modules that you complete on the way to the overall award. The behaviourists would argue against this, suggesting that the modular elements are more important. The theorists working with gestalt theory suggested that people learn how to solve whole situations by using a problem-solving approach to situations. Gestalt theory is based on the concept of insight, which has a specific meaning to this area of theory. Insight can be described as the perception of a situation that leads to a result or solution. The learner considers each element of a problem, and by using previous knowledge and experience, the solution becomes apparent. You might have considered a particular problem or issue at work, and by reflecting on your past experience or knowledge, you had a flash of inspiration of what worked for that situation; you will then apply this to your current issue. This theory could be problematic for people who find it difficult to visualise the whole or entire element of a problem – some people prefer to break things into smaller, more manageable pieces.

Cognitivism

The cognitivist theory places the student at the centre of the learning process. This theory focuses on how the student assimilates and organises knowledge. The cognitivists argue that students do not merely accept information, but they organise it and situate it in a manner that means something to them. Cognitivism relies on the skill of reflection and allowing the student to reflect on the information given to them, actively engaging the mind in relation to the themes that they are considering.

This theory may be problematic to apply to a situation where there are 20 or so students in the same classroom or learning scenario, as they will all have their own way of reflecting and assimilating information. However, in a learning situation where the student is the only person present – i.e. individual tutorial or personal learning session – this theory could be powerful and beneficial.

Humanism

The humanist theory was introduced in the 1960s as a reaction against behaviourism. It is quite different to previous theories as, arguably, it does not have the coherence of previously discussed theories. Humanist theorists argue that the actions of the student create the learning situation. The student's personality is central in that it allows the increase in autonomy that promotes successful learning. The learning process is structured around the goals that the students set for themselves and the social setting within which they operate. The humanists argue that setting one's own goals and learning are interlinked and natural processes that rely on the personality. They further argue that motivation for learning is key to the success and comes from within. This theory stresses that learning happens as a result of autonomy as opposed to control.

Learning in a humanist way is more likely to be successful if you are learning away from a classroom scenario, where there are no firm boundaries and structures and where you can be self-motivated and set your own goals. In terms of the MTL, as with any other accredited programme, there will be certain stipulations that you are unable to negotiate, for example, the learning outcomes, and the type of assessment, nor may you be able to negotiate a deadline for completion. However, the content and pace at which you learn may be more flexible.

Now that you have had a brief introduction to just some of the key theories, give some consideration to how you feel that you would learn most successfully. You may feel that by taking part in the MTL, you will use certain aspects of different theories, maybe as a result of how the modules in the MTL are delivered. For example, some modules may be delivered online, in which case you will identify a learning method that allows you to access the information appropriate for you. You may ask for telephone tutorials, or email tutorials. Similarly, if you attend group study sessions, you may draw on different learning skills. You are likely to be able to identify with at least some of the theory when considering your own learning style and methods.

A new approach to learning: a pragmatic alternative

This study skills guide will offer a pragmatic approach to learning. This approach is based on the personal feelings and the professional situation of the individual learner. The pragmatic alternative is dependent on you as the learner identifying how you can help to create a learning environment that is best for you, taking into account all those things going on in your life that vie for a piece of your time. These are discussed in more detail later in the book, but for now, as an example, try to give some consideration to the following: are you able to set aside a certain amount of time each week, or will you need to 'steal' short bursts of time in which you can read or write a few lines? Are you able to use the classroom in which you teach as a learning opportunity for yourself, or do you need to find a quiet area in order to take in information? Do you respond well to positive feedback or do you prefer to carry out the task without any critique from another person? It is argued that before any learning can take place, you need to feel safe, confident and positive about the learning process. The potential for you as a learner to feel threatened or intimidated needs to be recognised and any barriers to your learning excluded. You can influence this by reflecting on your feelings and being open and flexible to change, discuss your learning with colleagues and friends.

The pragmatic alternative being proposed offers a 'blended learning' approach, an aggre-gate of different learning techniques dependent on what time you have for learning. It is suggested that you base the vast majority of your learning in the classroom in which you teach, but support this by using other appropriate areas at home, work and university. Very few people these days have the opportunity to disengage from the frenetic pace of daily life in order to escape to a library or study centre. Office space is also at a premium, so it is unlikely that you have an office to yourself. So just where can you learn? Where can you study? Given that the MTL is based in the workplace, you will probably struggle to access traditional styles of study space. You may be able to use a quieter classroom for meetings with your mentor or coach, but the important thing is for you to identify an area in which you feel able to learn and study. Blended learning takes into account the challenges of accessing a learning area and therefore seeks to identify, in a flexible manner, the most effective learning environment. In a pragmatic sense this involves being open and adaptable to finding learning space. The following chapters discuss the practicalities of this approach in more detail.

Practical Task

Discuss what method of feedback from tutors, your study and work colleagues feel is appropriate. Identify their thoughts on how they learn best: from what learning situations are they most likely to learn? How does this compare to your own preferred style?

Using the literature suggested on the further reading list, identify the names of the theorists developing the theories explained here.

Summary

This chapter has offered the opportunity for you to address and identify with some of the theories and models of learning. It has suggested:
- a new 'blended' approach to learning, in which you 'drive' the types of learning that you will experience;
- that you negotiate your learning with tutors and supervisors;
- ways in which theory underpins different learning styles;
- that you will have adapted a certain individual learning style that is unique to you.

References and **Further reading**
Ahmed, S., Kilby, J., Lury, C., McNeill, M. and Skeggs, B. (2000) *Transformations: Thinking through feminism*. London: Sage.
Bloom, B.S. (1960) *Taxonomy of Educational Objectives1*. Cognitive Domain. David McKay.
Bush, T. and West-Burnham, J. (1994) *The Principles of Educational Management*. Harlow: Longman.
Dave, R. (1975) in Armstrong, R.J. et al. *Developing and Writing Behavioural Objectives*. Educators' Innovation Press.
Moon, J. (2004) *A Handbook of Reflective and Experiential Learning: Theory and Practice*. Abingdon: Routledge.
Murray, R. and Moore, S. (2006) *The Handbook of Academic Writing: A fresh approach*. Maidenhead: Open University Press/McGraw-Hill.
Reece, I. and Walker, S. (1997) *Teaching, Training and Learning: A practical guide* (third edn). Tyne and Wear: Business Education Publishers Limited.
Senge, P. (1990) *The Fifth Discipline*. London: Random House.

CHAPTER 2

Developing higher-level study skills

Chapter Objectives

By the end of this chapter, you should be able to:
- reflect on a variety of different study skills;
- have a greater understanding of the significance of motivation, time management and target setting;
- demonstrate how to get the most from attending a lecture, discussions with colleagues, problem-solving and practical activities such as role play;
- be able to apply different higher-level study skills to the MTL.

Links to standards
This chapter will help you to address the following professional teaching standards.

C3   Maintain an up-to-date knowledge and understanding of the professional duties of teachers and the statutory framework within which you work, and contribute to the development, implementation and evaluation of the policies and practice of your workplace, including those designed to promote equality of opportunity.

C7   Evaluate your performance and be committed to improving your practice through appropriate professional development.

C8   Have a creative and constructively critical approach towards innovation: being prepared to adapt your practice where benefits and improvements are identified.

C10 Have a good, up-to-date working knowledge and understanding of a range of teaching, learning and behaviour management strategies and know how to use and adapt them, including how to personalise learning to provide opportunities for all learners to achieve their potential.

C35 Review the effectiveness of your teaching and its impact on learners' progress, attainment and well-being, refining your approach where necessary.

C37 Establish a purposeful and safe leaning environment which complies with current legal requirements, national policies and guidance on the safeguarding and well-being of children and young people so that learners feel secure and sufficiently confident to make an active contribution to learning and to the school. Identify and use opportunities to personalise and extend learning through out-of-school contexts where possible making links between in-school learning and learning in out-of-school contexts.

P2   Have an extensive knowledge and understanding of how to use and adapt a range of teaching, learning and behaviour management strategies, including how to personalise learning to provide opportunities for all learners to achieve their potential.

> **P5** Have a more developed knowledge and understanding of your subject's curriculum areas and related pedagogy including how learning progresses within yourself.
>
> **P10** Contribute to the professional development of colleagues through coaching and mentoring, demonstrating effective practice, and providing advice and feedback.
>
> **E1** Be willing to take a leading role in developing workplace policies and practice and in promoting collective responsibility for their implementation.
>
> **E2** Research and evaluate innovative curricular practices and draw on research outcomes and other sources of external evidence to inform your own practice and that of colleagues.
>
> **E14** Contribute to the professional development of colleagues using a broad range of techniques and skills appropriate to your needs so that you demonstrate enhanced and effective practice.

Introduction

It might have crossed your mind to question the necessity of developing higher-level study skills; after all, as a teacher, you will probably have taken part in study of some sort, you may also have engaged in research or in developing new initiatives, all of which would have required you to have drawn on your learning and study skills. So, why is it now being suggested that you engage in the development at a higher level? Well, given that teaching is progressing to a master's-level profession, and given that my research to date has identified that some teachers experience difficulties when trying to understand the concept of master's-level study, it is highly likely that teachers will need some sort of informative study skills advice at the appropriate level to which they can refer as necessary.

Having already completed a programme that led to a teaching qualification, many experienced teachers feel that their professional development is complete. It is argued here that obtaining qualified teacher status is just the start, and once you have secured a teaching post, your professional development can begin.

This chapter will offer you the opportunity to develop an understanding of the types of skills required for studying at master's-level and in doing so it will identify methods and techniques by which to further develop and progress these skills, whether you are approaching this study from the perspective of someone who is participating on a course which awards QTS or if you are taking part in postgraduate study at master's level.

Motivation

The word 'motivation' originates from the Latin *movere* – 'to move'. A motive is therefore something that moves you into action. But, what is this thing we call 'motivation'? Why do you do something specific? Why do you feel attracted to certain things but not attracted to others?

The word motivation is suggestive of something or some energy within you that is moving you or driving you to do something. This energy could be fuelled by emotion, need, determination or some similar feeling that grows within you to the extent that you feel you need to act. Furthermore, the way in which you act is determined by this specific energy or motivation. Most people can galvanise themselves into action of some sort, but is this motivation? Adair (1996) for example, argued that in order to be truly motivated, you need to engage a 'will' and 'intent' to do something. There is a difference, albeit quite subtle, in the motivations you have to act in a certain way, and being motivated to act. As an example, consider the following scenario.

> *Maggie had been in the same job for five years and had been looking to move, either to another organisation or on promotion within the same organisation. Her motives to move were that she had felt she could perform most of the tasks, there were no longer any challenges, she had grown quite complacent in her current role, she wanted to progress and develop within her profession and she had recently divorced so she needed to provide herself financial security. However, she stayed within her original role; she did not have the motivation to move as the emotional and moral support she received from work managers and colleagues, particularly during her recent divorce, led to her not being motivated to leave that supportive environment.*

Motivation could be described then as a desire or will to do something that leads to an action that is meaningful.

Stick-and-carrot motivation is a concept where external stimuli influence the action. Does the donkey work better if prodded with a stick, or when a carrot is dangled in front of its nose? Do you work better and more effectively if there is some sort of negative threat of what might happen if you do not do something, or if there is a reward at the end of what you do successfully? For example, consider the following statements and decide in which scenario you are most likely to be successful.

- You have been asked by the head teacher to lead a project that will result in a group of children working in the local community with the local allotment holders' association. The head teacher has informed you that if this project is not successful the reputation of the school within the community will be severely impinged; she also reminded you that the chairman of the school governors is also the co-ordinator of the allotment holders' association and the original idea for this project was his.
- You have been asked by the head teacher to plan and implement a short presentation to school governors regarding a recent school trip that you organised to the recycling depot. The children who went on the trip then helped to prepare a recycling policy for the school. The head offered to pay for cover time for you in order that you could have two planning days the following week in retrospect, if this presentation went well.

Perhaps you are now able to determine if you work more effectively if offered a 'carrot', or if shown a 'stick'.

Conversely, many writings on motivation centre around Maslow's hierarchy of needs, in which it is suggested that a person is not motivated by external stimuli, but by a set of internal needs. If you are not familiar with Maslow's hierarchy of needs, it would be a good idea to develop an understanding of this before proceeding (Hayes, 2000).

In order to complete the MTL, you will need to develop a consistency of motivation to underpin your studies. Your tutors will help you and will provide certain motivators. However, the most important stimuli, be they external or internal, will need to come from you. My experience of working as a tutor in further and higher education has identified the fact that the most successful adult learners are those who have been able to keep motivated throughout. It might help to consider Table 2.1.

Table 2.1 Motivation and stimuli

Initial motivation The drive to register and engage in continuing professional development, in this instance the MTL	*Sources – External and/or internal* Government policy *Local requirement.* – school or organisational policy *Personal/professional* – the desire to improve practice and knowledge.
First step motivation The energy and drive that supports you through the early stages of the MTL	*Critical friendship* – a 'study buddy', a colleague or fellow student whose views you respect and who you can work with during the study for the MTL *Tutor* – your tutor will understand that you may need support with motivation on occasions throughout the programme *Family and friends* – talk to people about your study and gauge their response.
Second step motivation The 'staying power' momentum that will serve to keep you going through the longer term.	As above plus: • Personal developed strength • Reflecting on formative successes during primary stages of the programme, i.e. the development of confidence from passing modules along the way.
Third step motivation The momentum to progress to the next programme of learning	Government policy. *Tutor* – your tutor will be able to support you in identifying the next appropriate course *Local requirements* – you may be contractually obliged to continue studying or researching

adapted from Adair (1996)

Setting targets

It is likely that the MTL will be more manageable if you are able to divide it into smaller pieces. The fundamental fragmentation will have taken place during the validation of the award, in terms of the way in which the university developed and wrote the MTL. The overall structure of the MTL is designed in three, but within each phase there will be modular programmes. You will be given a set amount of time in which you will need to complete the work for a particular module. It is vital that you adhere to the deadlines that you are given. It is normally recommended to students that they identify the official deadline and then use a fortnight before as their deadline. For example, if your work needs to be handed in at 17.00hrs on Friday 28 January, then set your deadline as 14 January. This offers a safety net in case extra time is needed for unforeseen circumstances. It also offers both the student and tutor a window through which they can work through corrections or amendments.

Try to set yourself short-term targets for study. As you progress through the MTL you will need to develop a 'bank' of literature around your area of study and given that it is unlikely that you would be able to dedicate many hours to reading, try to set short-term study targets. The following list offers some ideas for short-term target setting for your reading.

- Read and understand a book chapter or journal paper each week.
- Attempt to record references to three to five authors each week.
- Be flexible in determining the amount of time and days you can set aside for study. For example, if you are normally able to use two evenings or half a day at weekend for study, don't be demoralised or demotivated if, on some occasions, you can't manage this, but be aware that you may need to put a bit extra in on the next occasion.
- When writing, aim to write a certain amount on each occasion. It is rare that you will be able to find the time to write an essay of 5,000 words in one sitting. So be realistic, and write 600–1,000 words per sitting. When I set out to write this book, it would have been an unrealistic target to try to write it all in a week or two, so I planned to write a chapter every one or two weeks.

It would be wrong to prescribe your study time – only you can do that, but it is felt that you are more likely to succeed if you pace yourself, seeking help from your tutor and/or coach if necessary.

Setting long-term targets can help in maintaining motivation and momentum. The ultimate long-term target is the achievement of a master's degree, and this alone could act as the motivation for some students. However, for others the completion of the first year, for example, is a better and more realistic long-term target. The completion of a term could also act as a long-term target. Charles Handy (1996, p172) talks of 're-chunking' time. By this he means that in order to get the best out of the time we have we need to 'recognise the realities' and arrange and plan our time accordingly, and where this applies to target-setting, it also relates to and leads on to the following section.

Time management

Managing your time effectively is one of the great challenges of modern life. Handy (1996, p22) reported that:

> *If we are to cope with the turbulence of life today, we must start by finding a way to organise it in our minds. Until we do that, we will feel impotent, a victim of events beyond our control or even our capacity to understand.*

In order to manage your time effectively, you will need to prioritise tasks. In taking part in the MTL you have added a set of study and learning tasks to your repertoire. You will need to identify time to perform these study tasks effectively. Your tutor will understand that you may have family and domestic commitments, you have probably got professional commitments and responsibilities, and now you have added another dimension in the shape of a master's degree to demand your time. However, your tutor is charged with supporting you in completing this award and therefore will expect that you will dedicate some priority to study. If you are sufficiently interested in a particular area, or if you have a particular passion about a part of your practice, you are more likely to find the time to study these areas further and you are less likely to resent giving time to study. It is evident (DfEE, 2001) that the government plans to encourage teachers to use the classroom as their own learning environment. Reflective learning and 'on the job' learning are discussed later in the book. However, when considering time management, it is important to be able to identify if time can be used while in class to perform study tasks. It is a good idea to keep a reflective study diary, in which you can make notes wherever you are. The diary need only to be for your use, so the notes you make will not be seen by anyone – it is an excellent means of recording situations or passages from books or journals. It is also another way of making good use of your time.

It is recommended that you inform as many people as possible about your study. In particular, your head teacher needs to know that you are taking part in the MTL. You need to have a conversation with the head teacher in which you can negotiate study time. Schools will not find it easy to provide cover for all teachers carrying out the MTL; however, if you don't ask and offer to negotiate some time, you may forgo something to which you were entitled. Talk to friends and family about your study time, and defend the time you set aside for study. You may need to make sacrifices, for example, on occasions you may have to finish an essay rather than attend a party with your partner. If you continually give less preference and priority to your study, don't be too upset if your friends, family and colleagues seem to give little credence to your study. If you turn down an invitation once or twice, people soon realise that you are serious about your development and begin to involve you in any event planning. You can normally pick up on postponed or lost social events, whereas you might find it difficult to pick up on a lost opportunity to do some reading or writing.

You might find it helpful to write down the times that you are able to study, for example in a diary or calendar style: that way, by looking back on the time that you have already committed to your study, you are probably more likely to invest more time to the project. This is another useful aspect of keeping a reflective or study diary.

Attending a lecture

When attending a lecture, it is advisable to do some reading around the subject prior to listening to the lecture: that way you will have some understanding of what is being said, rather than the lecture being the first time you have encountered the subject. Many people leave lectures disappointed that they were unable to fully appreciate and understand what was being addressed; this is often due to them not engaging with the subject beforehand. Another benefit of having some idea of the area of focus of a lecture is that you are more likely to be confident to put questions to the lecturer, and in doing that, you are more likely to get to grips with the subject.

During the lecture itself, there are a number of ways in which you can take information and knowledge from the lecture. The most obvious way is to listen to what is being said, and make notes that you will understand later when reading through. You could make notes based on what the lecturer is saying without really giving much thought to the implications of what is being said. The higher-level approach to this would require you to not simply to write down what is being said, but to think about the wider issues and give some thought to the implications and possible contradictions. That way you will be developing a more critical approach to attending a lecture and you will get more out of it. For example, think of how the issues apply to you or to your organisation, would they work in your practice? Why might they not work? You might be left wondering what if? or so what? It doesn't matter as long as you record your feelings in a way that makes sense to you at a later date. The way in which the lecture is delivered will make a big difference to the quality of information and knowledge that you get from the lecture; however, you have little control of the delivery, but you do have some control over your learning.

There may be handouts or notes given by the lecturer, these may or may not be helpful to you. Remember, we have different ways of assimilating information and in understanding. The notes that the lecturer has produced are their notes, and they make sense to them; there is no substitute for taking your own notes, written in a way that you will appreciate and understand.

If you are able, it is a good idea to attend several lectures on the same area or subject. This will offer you the opportunity to view the issues from different perspectives and to have the benefit of the view of more than one lecturer. Don't turn down an opportunity to attend a lecture simply because you have already experienced a lecture on the same or similar subject on a previous occasion.

Reading for study

Taking part in the MTL will require you to read widely. You will also need to identify a system of reading and of referencing what you have read. The earlier you do this, the better. There is nothing worse than reading an article in a book or journal in a library and not being able to refer to that article when you need to at a later stage of your study. There are several methods by which you can record what you have read and therefore begin to build a *bank of reference*.

- Notebook – keep a reference notebook within which you can record excerpts from books and journals and note the author, date and publication.
- Electronic file – keep a file on your computer that is purely for references and passages from books, papers and journals.
- Dictaphone or digital recorder – you can record information, author's name, etc., and then either download onto a computer or play back and record later. This method is particularly useful if you have little time and want to obtain as much information as possible in the time that you have. It does however, require you to spend time either downloading or transcribing at a later date.
- Index system – write your references and any excerpts on index cards and store in an index box.

Whatever method or methods you use, remember that it is your system so adapt it to suit your own style. The way in which you do this is not set in stone, so you can change it as necessary. The main information to record is: the passage of writing, author's name and initials, date on which the book or journal was published, page number of the passage you have recorded, title of book, journal and the title of the journal paper. You will also need to make a note of the publisher and where the publisher is located. This information is normally recorded on the first two pages of any book.

You may like to copy the chart in Table 2.2 to help you to set up a recording system.

Table 2.2 Reference system

Author's name:	Date of publication:	Title of book:	Title of paper in journal and title of journal:
Page number of account:	Publisher:	Place of publication:	Nature of account: Direct quote ☐ Summary ☐ Overview ☐
Account:			

You may need to develop different ways and methods of reading. You will not be able to read the entire contents of all the books that you access, therefore you will choose to read in a way that suits the task that you need to complete. The following bullet points identify different methods of reading and the tasks that are appropriate to that style.

- *Rapid scan*: To check what you are reading. A quick scan is all that is necessary as you only need to identify if the book is the right one, current and right for the task. Will you need to access all the contents or just a few? Is the book or journal article written in a way that you can understand what is being said?
- *Selective testing*: Read the content in more detail; you may read the introduction in some depth, or a large part of it. Study the chapter headings and skim over a few pages in selected chapters. The question in your mind when selective testing is always: *can I understand what is written and are the contents suitable for my study?* Test parts of the beginning of select chapters to identify if they apply to your work.
- *Skimming*: When you skim-read you are making a quick judgement about the book or article. You need to try to get a general idea of what the book is about, what are the key areas and what argument does the author propose. Skimming involves reading a few sentences here and there, not in any great detail, and not trying to analyse the text.
- *Focused search*: You will use this method when you need to find out a specific piece of information. For this you will go to the contents page or index, locate the page on which your information sits and record it. The important thing here is that you don't get bogged down or sidetracked into reading large sections of the book. Once you have identified what it is you want, put the book or journal down and move on.
- *Selecting sections*: When you need to concentrate on one section, paragraph, chapter, etc. This is the only part of the book that you'll need, so again, don't get sidetracked into reading too much of other sections. Read the part that you need, take any notes and move on. This method does require you to be quite disciplined and controlled.
- *Focused study reading*: This is the reading that you will do to fully understand the content, and is the most common method for this level of study. You will need to apply yourself completely to what you are reading and therefore may need to read in silence and without distraction. You may need to make notes while you are reading. You will need to understand what the author is saying, which argument they take and why.

Adapted from Cottrell (2005)

It is suggested throughout this book that you keep a reflective study diary. In terms of reading, this is really important and you will be able to note down passages or titles of reading material that you access. During the MTL you will be given reading lists. These will contain details of suggested reading texts. The list will not be exhaustive and you will not be expected to read the entire contents of each book, but you will be required to access each of the texts.

When reading it is also important that you question what you have read. Ask yourself – 'What is the main point here?' and 'So what'? Make sure that you have understood all the arguments and conclusions.

Discussions with colleagues – critical friend

Talking about your study is a really good way to cement it in your own mind. Discuss your ideas and study methods with colleagues and friends, ask them for their views and thoughts. You might find several other people share a similar study theme to your own. Some might contradict your view, it is only by talking about it that you will identify the different approaches between colleagues. You may discover that you are able to relate to one or two key people who understand the area that you are studying and can offer appropriate suggestions to you. Critical friendship can develop from relationships such as this. The main thing to consider before entering into a critical friendship is that you must completely trust the person with whom you have the friendship and you would not be offended when they offered you critical appraisal of your work. Costa and Kallick (1993) suggested that the role of critical friends has been introduced to educational establishments in order that individuals can be provided with feedback. This is really important as it gives you another perspective of your work and can help you to see yourself in a different way. Similarly, Andreau et al. (2003) suggested a critical friend model as being a situation where members examine each other's practice, giving feedback to each other in order to enhance their work. The key phrase here is to enhance work: critical friendship would be quite obstructive and potentially damaging if it were not carried out in order to improve and enhance. Bloom (1999) found that critical friend groups can allow members to help each other in examining their work and making changes as required. Given that you will be completing the MTL with other colleagues, it may be appropriate to set up a critical friends group – particularly if you are new to studying at this level. Do not underestimate the benefit of using colleagues to critique your work. Day (1999, p144) claims that:

> Critical friendship is based upon practical partnerships entered into voluntarily, which presuppose a relationship between equals and are rooted in a common task of shared concern. The role of the critical friend is to provide support and challenge within a trusted relationship.

Problem-solving

A problem-solving approach can be useful when studying in terms of being able to tackle challenges and problems in a rational and systematic manner. Learning by problem-solving normally begins with an unstructured and often disorganised problem or set of problems and requires the learner to think about, plan and develop solutions and in so doing, gain an insight into the theory that underpins the problem. During the course of your practice, you will experience problems and challenging situations that you can use as learning opportunities for the MTL. This will enable you to use your own classroom practice as the base for your learning.

* Identify the problem.
* Consider different ways of tackling it.

- Plan and try out your chosen method for solving the problem.
- Review the situation – has the problem been solved successfully?

There are some useful skills to develop that will help you to learn by this method effectively.

- Effective questioning – ask appropriate questions and be prepared to write down notes on the answers received.
- Reflect on your own practice – what are your strengths? what are your weaker areas? What situations do you deal with effectively and which provide challenges to you? Try to be critical about yourself, but remember, being critical does not mean being negative, it is a positive exercise that allows you to look at the subject as a whole, a 'warts and all' approach to viewing something.
- Prioritise – if you are faced with a set of problems or a concurrent set of issues that you need to address simultaneously, you will probably need to prioritise the order in which you address the problems. This will involve attaching a value to each of the problems and systematically working through the problems in the order in which you have categorised them. As an example, you will need to address several learning outcomes for each of the MTL modules, but prioritising them in an order that makes sense to you, and in a way that you can address them, will make achieving them more straightforward.

Role play

Role play can be an effective practical learning technique that provides an opportunity for learners to experience meaningful interaction, in a situation that you may not normally experience as part of your job. You may use role play in your own classroom practice in order to identify how your learners react when put into different scenarios. You will therefore acknowledge that role play is only valuable if the actors can reflect on what they have done and why they performed in the way that they did. Creating a successful role play exercise depends on careful and robust planning, Your own learning can benefit from observing these role play activities by reflecting on the effectiveness of your planning and implementation. You may decide to be a player alongside your pupils, in which case you would be able to offer another dimension to your learning. Given that role play is largely a practical activity, it is suggested that you allow time immediately following the exercise in which you can write your observations and reflections and other learning notes. The bullet points below set out the key themes when using role play.

- Careful planning and preparation are key to the success of role play.
- Place the actors in appropriate roles.
- Set the scene for the cast in a clear and succinct manner.
- Identify what it is you want to get from the role-play exercise.
- Make notes of your reflections and learning as soon as possible after the exercise.
- Review and evaluate the role play and be critical with the outcome.

Practical Task

Carry out a role-play situation as part of your classroom practice. Identify your own learning as a result of this. Plan the role-play scenario to enable you to use a problem-solving approach with your pupils following the exercise. Some examples of themes are as follows.

- Walking in the woods.
- School trip via coach to seaside.
- Trip to the zoo.
- Visit to an art gallery.

Case studies

A case study is often associated with research and this book will address the research element of case studies in Chapters 5 and 6. However, case studies can also be valuable to your learning. Given that case studies offer a particular example or instance of a specific situation that is used to demonstrate a more general issue (Cohen et al., 2000), it is evident that by reading a case study you would be able to reflect on how your practice or learning could compare to the issues within the case study. They normally provide examples of reality in terms of placing people and situations within the context of their work. Case studies often attempt to portray the realness of situations, but in order to learn from them, it is essential that you place yourself and your own situation within that of the case study

Case studies are used throughout this book in order to provide you with the opportunity to acknowledge how you might act if placed in a certain situation. They also enable you to compare your practice to that of the actors within the case study. To obtain the maximum benefit from a case study, you will need to ask yourself questions about the situation; don't take things for granted, try to look behind what is being expressed. The case study below offers you the opportunity to do just that and the tasks following provide you with some questions regarding the situation.

Case Study

A group of teachers were taking part in a professional development session. The session was focusing on ethical dilemmas and equality. Most of the teachers had examples to share with the group who offered different perspectives to the examples depending on their own practice. The tutor leading the group gave each the following scenario.

A father and his son were driving along the road on a sunny day in late autumn, the sun was therefore quite low in the sky, making driving quite difficult. The road was also wet has it had been raining and the sun was reflecting off the road surface. As they approached a level crossing the father had to swerve quickly to avoid an oncoming car, this resulted in the car crashing into a wall and the boy being severely injured. The emergency services were called to the scene, the boy had to be cut free from the car. On arrival at the hospital the boy was taken straight to the emergency theatre where the surgeon announced; *'That's my son on the table'*.

The teachers were then asked how this could be and after some considerable time one of the groups had managed to identify that the surgeon was the boy's mother. This scenario was interesting as the groups initially automatically assumed that the surgeon was the boy's father.

Reflective Task

Imagine that you were one of the teachers taking part in the case study above. What methods could you employ to work out the situation? What factors would impact on the outcome that you reached? Now reflect on your own practice and development and give some thought to the most effective methods of study for your own purpose.

Summary

This chapter has identified how you can begin to develop higher-level study skills. It has provided ideas and suggestions for you in the following areas.

- Motivation – what are your motivators? What demotivates you?
- Time management – how do you make the best use of your study time?
- Target-setting – short-term and long-term targets.
- Getting the best from attending a lecture.
- Making the most of reading for your study.
- Critical friendship.
- Case studies.
- Problem-solving.

Throughout the chapter you have been encouraged to reflect on your own practice and learning and identify ways of enabling your learning to take place while fulfilling your role as a teacher.

References and Further reading
Adair, J. (1996) *Effective Motivation*. London: Pan Macmillan.
Andreau, R., Canos, L., De Juana, S., Manresa, E. Rienda, L. and Tari, J. (2003) Critical friends: a tool for quality improvement in universities. *Quality assurance in education.*, 11, (1): 31–6.

Bloom, B. (1999) Critical friends group in pursuit of excellence. *Mt. Airy Times Express*. 17 March 1999.

Boud, D. and Garrick, J. {eds) (1999) *Understanding Learning at Work*. Abingdon: Routledge.

Cohen, L., Mannion, L. and Morrison, K. (2000) *Research Methods in Education,* (5th edn) Abingdon: Routledge.

Costa, A. and Kallick, B. (1993) Through the lens of a critical friend. *Educational Leadership*. October, 1993: 49–51.

Cottrell, S. (2005) *Critical Thinking Skills*. London: Palgrave-Macmillan.

Day, C. (1999) *Developing Teachers: The challenges of lifelong learning*. Abingdon: Falmer Press.

Department of Education and Employment (DfEE) (2001) *Learning and Teaching: A strategy for professional development*. Green Paper. London: DfEE.

Handy, C. (1996) *Beyond Certainty*. London: Arrow.

Hayes, N. (2000) *Foundations of Psychology*. (3rd edn) London: Thompson Learning.

Jarvis, P., Holford, J. and Griffin, C. (2003) *The Theory and Practice of Learning*. (2nd edn) Abingdon: RoutledgeFalmer.

CHAPTER 3

Developing higher-level academic writing skills

Chapter Objectives

This chapter will identify ways in which you can develop your writing skills. It will offer the opportunity for you to build on your current academic writing style in order to be able to present essays at the level required of the MTL. By the end of this chapter you should be able to:
* plan, develop and structure an essay;
* develop a practical understanding of the Harvard referencing system;
* demonstrate a writing style appropriate to the MTL.

Links to standards
This chapter will help you to address the following professional teaching standards.

C2   Hold positive values and attitudes and adopt high standards of behaviour in your professional role.
C3   Maintain an up-to-date knowledge and understanding of the professional duties of teachers and the statutory framework within which they work, and contribute to the development, implementation and evaluation of the policies and practice of your workplace, including those designed to promote equality of opportunity.
C7   Evaluate your performance and be committed to improving your practice through appropriate professional development.
C10 Have a good up-to-date working knowledge and understanding of a range of teaching, learning and behaviour management strategies and know how to use and adapt them, including how to personalise learning to provide opportunities for all learners to achieve their potential.
P2   Have an extensive knowledge and understanding of how to use and adapt a range of teaching, learning and behaviour management strategies, including how to personalise learning to provide opportunities for all learners to achieve their potential.

Introduction

When you are asked to write an essay, the first thing you will probably think about is how long the essay needs to be. Some commentators offer the argument that effective writing can only take place when the author is inspired; however, you might not have the time to wait for inspiration to befall you, so you will need to find ways of gaining inspiration, as essays that you write for the MTL may well have a word count and deadline attributed to them. You shouldn't dwell too much on the word count initially, but focus on getting started and the content of your work. The phrase 'to write an essay' is, strictly speaking, quite misleading, because the actual writing is something that you will do once you have planned, prepared and read for your essay, and is very often the part that takes the least amount of time, depending on how you plan and prepare your work.

This chapter will enable you to further develop your essay-writing skills and will offer you the opportunity to gain confidence in writing. It will suggest ways of writing that will be appropriate to the MTL.

What is meant by the term 'essay'? It is defined in the Collins English dictionary as *a short piece of writing on one particular subject that is written by a student.* In the context of the MTL, this could therefore be: a reflective account, assignment report, a research report or something similar. The assessment criteria of the MTL will identify the type of essay you will need to complete and your tutor will help you to develop this. The planning and design of your essay will fundamentally be the same, no matter what the structure. The detail of content depends on the actual subject and argument that you take. This chapter will address the areas of planning, design and development in detail.

Reflective Task

Read through some papers from education journal articles. Don't worry about the subject – in fact, it is probably best if you select a few articles that have been written about a subject that you know very little about, as you are going to critique these papers. You won't need to write anything down, just read the articles and reflect on what they are trying to say. What does the introduction tell you about the work? Is it understandable? Are you motivated to read the entire piece? Is the essay well organised? Has the author achieved what was set out in the title and introduction?

Identifying an appropriate topic

The main theme of your essay is likely to be dictated by the assessment criteria of the MTL modules; however, you will probably need to select a focus or argument for your essay. This stage in the development of your essay is crucial. You need to be confident and comfortable with the area that will form the focus of your essay. Once you fully understand the theme and your particular take on this, you can begin to plan for reading and carrying out any research that will help you to complete the work. Use the assessment requirements of each of the modules to help you to identify the theme and focus for your essay. Check out the examples below of assessment guidelines and essay titles that emanated from them.

> *Assessment guideline*: Demonstrate how your professional development has impacted on the organisation within which you practice.
> *Essay title*: A leadership journey: How professional development has helped the school improvement plan.

> *Assessment guideline*: Identify an area of innovation and critically analyse how this has impacted on your practice.
> *Essay title*: Using the interactive whiteboard: The pros and cons of embedding technology in the curriculum.

> *Assessment guideline*: Carry out a work-based project focusing on an area of need within your practice.
> *Essay title*: An action research study to identify the effectiveness of peer review at Key Stage 3.

The assessment criteria or guidelines set out a reasonably general area for your assignment or essay. You need to use this as a framework within which you identify a specific theme or focus that you can develop. Choose a focus that you are interested in, and to which you have good access. Your tutor will help you to do this. Discuss your ideas with colleagues and managers; they may be able to help you to refine your focus. It is advisable to stick to the same theme throughout your MTL. The reason is that you will begin to build a bank of knowledge and data from the very first module; if you then decide to look at very different areas for each module you complete, you will be making more work for yourself in terms of reading and researching these different areas, whereas if you stick to a central theme, you can further develop your knowledge on this theme as you progress through the modules.

Have a look at the two pathways in Table 3.1 and try to identify which route provides the more focused study opportunity.

Pathway 1 has CPD and leadership and management as a focal point throughout the degree. Therefore the teacher taking this pathway would be able to start building a data bank of references and knowledge around these areas. This teacher is more likely to develop a considerable knowledge around the areas of CPD and management by the time they reach the final module, and they are likely to be able to identify with key authors and offer their perspectives on the specific areas. In general the teacher following this pathway is more likely to feel that they have a certain authority to speak on the area of CPD in a leadership and management context.

Pathway 2 does not have a central theme, and therefore, the teacher taking this route would need to read on areas of: art and Italian art, behaviour for learning, English as a second language, mentoring, ICT, design and technology curriculum, gifted and talented curriculum, Key Stage 3, interactive whiteboard and children with autism. This produces a really difficult task, and teachers completing this pathway will need to begin to read on very

Table 3.1. Pathways comparison

	Module 1	Module 2	Module 3	Module 4	Module 5	Module 6	Module 7	Module 8
Pathway 1	A comparison of how leadership skills developed in my previous job in business management has impacted on my current role as a teacher	Supporting the school improvement plan: A reflective account of the implementation of a CPD strategy for staff	Managing the implementation of change: A critique of skills required to introduce a new CPD strategy	A comparison of leadership theory: Analysing how this impacts on my practice	A work-based study to identify what influences teachers' decisions to engage with CPD	A case study demonstrating how INSET can impact on classroom practice	What influences teachers decisions to disengage from CPD? A small-scale research study	The development of a toolbox of skills for CPD managers in school
Pathway 2	A portfolio of evidence and reflection on leading a school visit to the Italian art galleries	A critique of the school policy on behaviour for learning	Managing the implementation of a policy to aid integration of foreign pupils	What makes an effective mentor?	Using ICT in design and technology	A case study analysing the introduction of a gifted and talented policy	Strengths and limitations of using interactive whiteboard at Key Stage 3	An action research study to highlight key areas to consider when introducing resources for children with autism

different areas for each module. It could also create difficulties and challenges for the teacher, as when they reach the final module, which is likely to be a research project, they will need to read extensively on a subject that they have not previously studied.

Choose the topic of your module carefully, don't make things too difficult for yourself. Ask your tutor for advice whenever necessary. Don't worry too much about the actual title at the beginning of your essay, very often the title is the last thing that you do and something which comes from the essay, rather than driving the work.

Planning the essay

Spend time in careful and robust planning: the whole project depends on this. If you neglect this stage, you run the risk of running out of time and producing a piece of work that is disorganised and unstructured. Decide how you want to shape your essay, bearing in mind that it needs to address the following areas.

* Introduction.
* Literature review.
* Main body – main argument.
* Conclusion and discussion.
* References.

Develop a plan to assist you in the completion of your essay, setting time aside for: reading, obtaining data and evidence, visiting libraries (if you need postal loans or inter-library loans allow extra time), preparing notes and the final writing. If you keep a reflective diary, you can utilise this to assist you with planning.

When setting out to begin the plan, try to look at the general theme from different angles, not just your own perspective. It helps if you sit with a blank piece of paper with the theme written in the centre and let your imagination flow around the topic, write down everything that comes into your head however insignificant it may appear at first glance. The diagram in Figure 3.1 is an example.

The central theme is 'Managing change' and written around the theme are several related ideas and random thoughts, some of which will be more useful and usable than others. Once you have completed this, leave it for a day or two, but keep thinking about your central theme and allow your own practice to feed into your thoughts regarding your essay plan. Make random notes in your study diary or notebook. When you go back to your plan, cross out any previous notes that you feel are irrelevant and add other notes as appropriate. Leave the plan again for a couple of days, but again, keep thinking about it and chat to colleagues about your thoughts. When you come back to your plan for a second time, make further amendments as necessary. The plan is now ready to be transferred onto another piece of paper, either electronically or in hard copy. This will then give you a basic plan to develop your essay.

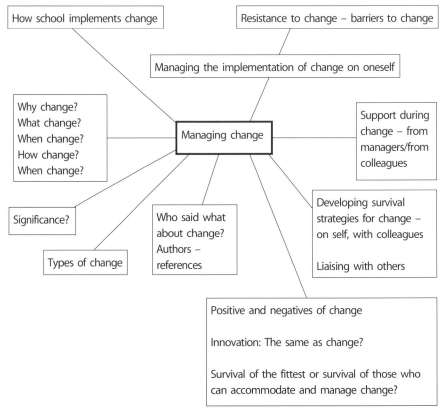

Figure 3.1 Example of essay-planning diagram

Practical Task

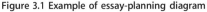

Start with an empty A4 piece of paper. In the centre, write down a subject or theme that interests you. Then spend about 15–20 minutes just writing anything – all random thoughts, that come into your head about this subject. Then leave this for at least a day. Come back to this piece of paper and add other notes to it. Leave it again for a couple of days, but start to think about your theme. Come back to the paper again and this time start to look at your notes around the theme and identify links between them. You will probably decide that some notes are not significant, therefore cross them out and concentrate on the few notes that you have been able to link and expand on these.

On a blank piece of A4 write your theme again in the centre, but this time only write the areas that you have selected from your initial random thoughts.

Draw a chart detailing the outline of an essay around this basic plan.

Reading and reviewing the literature

Using your essay plan, identify the areas of reading that you will need to access. From the managing change example given on the previous page, some of the areas of reading might be as follows.

* Managing the implementation of change in education.
* Managing oneself when change is introduced.
* Barriers to change.
* Methods of introducing change.
* Curriculum change.
* Change in government policy affecting education.
* Actors or stakeholders involved in change.
* Authors – John Elliott, DCSF, Charles Handy, Bush and West-Burnham.

Managing literature is really important as you can easily get swamped in information and data. Be disciplined when reading and try to stick to your plan, Campbell et al. (2004) agreed with this by suggesting that there is a danger when adopting an unorganised approach to reviewing literature that you will lose any structure to your study.

Once you have developed your plan and reading list, you can begin to build a data bank of information. It is useful to have copies of your reading list with you, in case you are able to go to a library or you have some time to access the internet. Use the librarians and learning resource staff to help you to identify suitable texts. Your tutor will also help, and you may have been given a reading list by your tutor, which you can use along with your own. The previous chapter offered methods of reading and referencing from texts, so please refer to this as necessary.

The following list will help you to understand some of the different vehicles for information.

* Books. Remember that a book is probably more out of date than a journal. Books take longer to write and publish and are therefore more likely to contain information that is not as current as a journal that is published monthly or biannually. Books however, will be invaluable at offering well-referenced well-researched information authored by experienced and knowledgeable professionals.
* Journals. These are reasonably up-to-date publications that contain reviewed papers and articles. Journals will normally adopt a particular perspective or angle. Current copies and a selection of back copies will be available in a library.
* Newspapers can offer current and applicable information to support your work and each may have a different perspective, which will help you to critique your work in terms of what is being discussed currently.
* Internet articles can be accessed via your own private search or via the university's virtual learning environment (VLE). It is important to acknowledge that anything can be publicised on the internet, therefore you will need to ensure that the information you take from the internet is from a reputable source, for example an electronic journal.

- Government literature and legislation. An extremely useful source of information as this is from where most organisational policy emanates.

The focus of your study will determine the depth at which you read the literature. If you are new to study and therefore new to the MTL, you will be somewhat comforted to know that experienced researchers and authors also struggle to focus on specific texts from the magnitude of literature that appears to be available (Blaxter et al., 1996). If you are reading alongside a colleague, don't worry if they seem to be able to extract information from literature that you find difficult: we all read and assimilate information in different ways, and therefore different author styles will appeal to different people. If you find a particular text difficult to read, you will also struggle to understand that text, so don't waste time trying to interpret, leave that text and go on to the next. It is very tempting for you as a teacher to think that your tutors and colleagues expect you to be able to understand at a particular level. Texts that are written at a high academic level may not be appropriate to everyone, so don't lose heart or confidence if you feel these texts are too difficult to understand, find authors that write at a level at which you are comfortable. You can always develop your reading skills as you progress with the MTL and with your continuing professional development in general.

Developing and structuring an argument

You will need to provide a focus for your writing. This, as has been previously discussed, could be as a result of the assessment criteria within the MTL programme; however, it may be that you need to identify a particular focus or argument yourself. You will use your reading and planning in order to form a focus that is relevant to your needs. The assessment criteria for the particular module of the MTL that you are completing may require you to do certain things, as in the following examples.

Demonstrate

The assessment might ask you to demonstrate how you would do something. It is a term normally associated with practical activity; however it is often used in essay assignment tasks to enable you to write about how you would do something. You will be expected to write about your thought process and any consequences. For example: *Demonstrate an understanding of health and safety issues in the classroom.* You could write about your awareness of the Health and Safety at Work Act and how this legislation is adhered to in the organisation and in your classroom. You might write about risk assessments, you could even incorporate a risk assessment as part of your evidence. You would be demonstrating an understanding by writing of the benefits of having a health and safety awareness about certain activities and you might also decide that there are some drawbacks or limitations – write about these as well.

Critically analyse

Critical analysis is discussed in more detail later in the book; however, it will crop up as an assessment criterion as being able to show true critical and analytical skills when writing is really what mastery is all about. When you critically analyse something, you weigh up the situation in terms of the negatives and positives. You will say what is beneficial about the situation and what is limited, and why. Analysing something involves taking it to pieces, addressing the fragments and formulating an argument or stand around the issues you have discovered. For example: *Critically analyse your leadership and management style*. You could begin by identifying what your style is according to a particular model. Say what you think you are good at and why; give examples. Say what you are less comfortable with and why; give examples. How could you improve? What would the implications be? Refer to the model and dissect the detail, say how your style either reflects these or how it contradicts them. Justify your argument with reference to other literature. Ask yourself the following questions: how does my leadership style impact on the learners? Justify this with examples; how does my leadership style impact on the organisation? Again justify with examples; and finally, how is my leadership style influenced by the curriculum?

Identify

When you identify something, you are saying that you know about it, that you have been able to discover a certain thing. Identifying your knowledge is very similar to demonstrating your knowledge, in that you will say how and why something happens or a situation occurs. In offering an identification of something you are saying to the reader, *Look, this is what I know about this, and this is how I know; I am also aware of these implications and issues surrounding the situation*. For example: *Identify the main considerations when planning and implementing a school visit abroad*. You would initially write about the planning, how the children were selected, costs, transport arrangements, etc. You would offer reasons why this might not be straightforward. You would need to say who else was involved and how sharing the planning either helped or hindered the process. You will need to say that you are aware of the administration and health and safety implications and describe these. You might want to include in the appendix a sample of your work as evidence. You would write about the implementation of the trip in much the same way.

Construct an argument

When you are asked this, you need to be able to show that you understand a particular area or situation and that you have taken a particular stance. Justify why you have taken this approach. When asked to construct an argument, you cannot 'remain on the fence', you must show that you can argue. Arguing does not need to be negative, it shows that you have a particular view or belief about something and that you are prepared to come out and talk about it. You must, however, strongly support all the perspectives with reference to practice and literature. You are saying that you believe this to be the case because … For example: *Construct an argument regarding the government's decision to make teaching a master's-level profession*. Let us assume that you believe it is a positive decision. You will argue that teaching needs to be a master's-level profession because…you might say that you concur with the government in terms of it increasing the status of teaching, or that it ensures teachers of the highest calibre will be teaching the country's children. You must, however, acknowledge the counter-argument. Why might the MTL be seen in a negative light? Why are some teachers reluctant when it comes to CPD at master's-level?

Reflect on

When asked to reflect, you can either reflect on something, a situation or policy for example, or you can reflect on your action. Schön (1991) discovered that practitioners reflect both in and on the action that they take. When writing about your reflections, you will need to document how you felt, and why. What made you feel that way? Do other people feel differently? Why might this be? Being reflective on paper is similar to looking into the mirror in order to gain the reflection of your face. When you look in the mirror, the reflection you get back is a 'warts and all' picture, and so it is with writing reflectively: you need to give a 'warts and all' view of your reflections on a particular subject. For example: *Reflecting on your own study, provide an account of the influences on your decision to engage with the MTL.* Your reflections might include some initial reservations from partners or your spouse. You may have had some doubts on your own ability or stamina. Alternatively, you may have felt coerced to complete it due to pressure from colleagues or managers. Ask yourself questions such as: Why did you feel this way? Did your feelings change? Providing a reflective account is entirely personal and often subjective, because it is asking for feelings, beliefs and values.

Develop an understanding of

When you are asked to develop an understanding, you need to inform the reader of your starting point, in terms of your knowledge. Once this has been established, you can then detail how your understanding has developed: this may have been a gradual process and would probably be dependent on your reading and training. Say how you have developed and how this has impacted on and influenced your practice. You will also need to refer to related literature as this will support your development and widen your understanding. For example: *Develop an understanding of how ICT can enhance the learner's experience.* You will begin by saying what your early understanding of ICT was. How you use it in the classroom, or how it is used in the school is important as is your approach to how you began to develop your knowledge of ICT. Tell the reader what aided your development and how you have been able to use your extended knowledge in the classroom. You may have learnt about new innovations, for example, virtual learning environments, e-portfolios, online databases and interesting websites.

Evaluate

When you are asked to evaluate something, you are required to review and look over a particular area and make a judgement of the effectiveness of this area. You need to be able to identify how the area you are evaluating has evolved and what has happened during the process, but the key to evaluation is placing a value and reaching a judgement on the outcome. Your evaluation may result in the identification of problem areas or shortcomings; alternatively, you may uncover examples of excellent practice. For example: *Evaluate the introduction of a behaviour policy which focuses on a zero tolerance approach*. You would describe the policy and identify why it was necessary to offer the reader a context for the rest of the essay. The focus of your writing would be to offer judgement, supported by evidence from practice and literature, on the effectiveness of the policy. The reader will need to be informed about zero tolerance, and what the alternatives may be. Your evaluation might suggest how the policy could be further embedded.

Writing your essay

If you have followed the suggested methods so far, you will already have begun to write your essay, in terms of the planning and citing texts. What is being referred to here is the draft of the final piece of work that you will submit for assessment. One of the main barriers to beginning to write your final piece of work is procrastination or convincing yourself that there are other things that you should be doing instead. Included in Table 3.2 below are some of the more common reasons.

Table 3.2 Main barriers to getting started

1	I just can't get motivated
2	I don't even know 5,000 words – let alone write them
3	I've never written at this level before
4	I'm too tired
5	It's not quiet enough
6	I've only got 20 minutes
7	I should really do the housework
8	I should really wash the car
9	I don't really feel too well
10	I'll do it at the weekend
11	I can't be bothered to fire the computer up for just 20 minutes
12	It all seems too difficult
13	I shouldn't need to have to do this – how will it make me a better teacher?
14	I didn't want to do the MTL anyway
15	I've never written an essay before
16	I need to finish this marking first
17	I've been busy all day at work, why should I start doing more now I'm at home?
18	Days off should be just that. I shouldn't be working on this. Rest and recuperation will be more beneficial to me in the long run
19	Staring for too long at the computer screen gives me a headache
20	I'd rather take the dog for a walk (even in the rain!)

There will be hundreds more reasons for not writing. If you find yourself trying to justify your decision not to carry out any writing, try to come up with ten reasons why you should make the effort. What would the consequences be of not completing: (a) your writing, (b) the module and (c) the MTL? It is sometimes more beneficial to promise to do 15 minutes, and no more. You will probably find that in doing 15 minutes, you carry on to do more anyway, and even if you don't, you will have done a quarter of an hour of writing that you could have missed.

When you begin to write, it is very unlikely that your initial writing will be the final and polished piece of work that you submit. It is more likely that it will be a draft, ripe for amendment and change depending on what your tutor suggests. It is therefore easier to use a word processor, as you can add and remove words and sentences more easily. You can also copy and paste chunks of work as appropriate and between texts.

Murray (2002, p11) suggested that you can develop skills that enable you to 'write to order'; she further identified that writing speedily and spontaneously can have the benefit of stimulating enthusiasm and negating self-doubt. Similarly, King (2000) indicated that writing quickly can serve to maintain stimulus and enthusiasm and therefore defend against the self-doubt that is so often only too keen to creep in.

When writing essays to satisfy the assessment criteria for the MTL, it is likely that you will have to adhere to a word count. For master's-level study, this is normally 5,000 words per 20 master's-level credits. Assuming then that you need to write a 5,000-word essay, it will be more manageable if you divide the word count up across the sections of your work as follows, for example.

- Introduction – 500 words approx.
- Literature review- 1,500 words approx.
- Main body of text and focus – 2,500 words approx.
- Conclusion – 500 words approx.

Introduction

The introduction is the section where you are telling the readers what you are doing, why and how. It should include the central aims of your study. Your introduction should identify how you have addressed the assessment criteria of the module. Remember that the first sentence of your essay is really important as you will need to try to engage the reader at this stage. The shape of the introduction is also important as it brings the reader into your writing and provides the link to the main body of the text. Figures 3.2 and 3.3 illustrate two shapes into which you can fit an introduction paragraph.

Literature review

The literature review is the section where you identify the literature that you have addressed and understood in respect of your essay. You will demonstrate here who the key contributors are in the field of your study. You will identify what they said that was of significance to your own work. This is your opportunity to inform the reader that you are familiar with

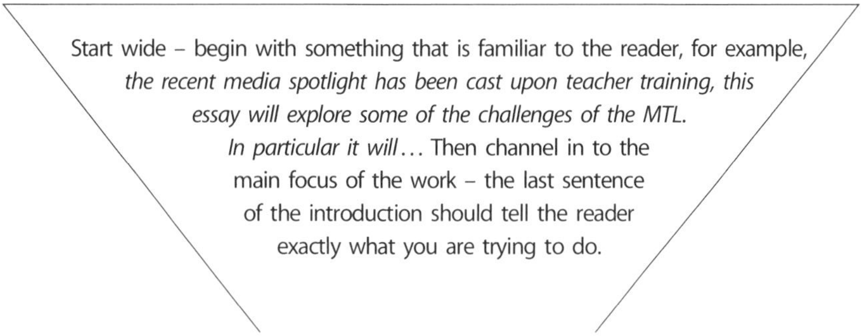

Start wide – begin with something that is familiar to the reader, for example, *the recent media spotlight has been cast upon teacher training, this essay will explore some of the challenges of the MTL. In particular it will…* Then channel in to the main focus of the work – the last sentence of the introduction should tell the reader exactly what you are trying to do.

Figure 3.2. Introduction model 1

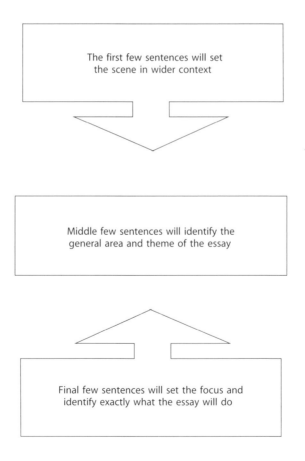

The first few sentences will set the scene in wider context

Middle few sentences will identify the general area and theme of the essay

Final few sentences will set the focus and identify exactly what the essay will do

Figure 3.3 Introduction model 2

certain arguments in the field and that your own area is worthy of study. The literature review is where you can add to the existing field of information and knowledge. Be careful not to simply quote from other works but analyse what is being said and apply it to the context of your study. Silverman (2000, p226) offered the following advice on the literature review.

There are four misconceptions of the literature review.

- It is done just to display that you know the area.
- It is easier to do than your data analysis chapters.
- It is boring to read and to write.
- It is best 'got out of the way' at the start of your work.

The literature review:

- should combine knowledge with critical thought;
- involve hard work but can be exciting to read;
- should mainly be written after you have completed any data analysis.

Main body of the text

This is the area of the essay where you demonstrate any research methodology and findings, or where you describe and analyse the central theme or focus. The following chapters focus on the research process and will go into this area in more depth. You can complete an essay without taking part in any empirical data collection, by identifying a focus and critically evaluating the literature surrounding this. Where this is the case, the middle sections of your essay will allow you to describe the focus in detail and offer arguments around this. You would also need to demonstrate how any issues described impact on or influence your practice. Remember that the MTL is a work-based master's degree and therefore you will need to refer to your practice throughout the programme.

If your essay is a critical reflective account, this section will form the main body of reflection. In this case you will identify what you did, why you did it and how you performed the task. You will need to show that you were able to stand back from the situation and analyse it from other perspectives, for example, what would have happened if...? What were the positives of what happened and why were they positive? What were the negatives and why were they negative? How could you have performed this in another way? What would the implications be for you? What would the implications be for the organisation?

Conclusion

The conclusion will draw together the essay and demonstrate the findings. This is where the author identifies how these findings can impact on wider issues, and lead to further development. The conclusion can also highlight areas of concern. It is good writing practice for the conclusion to pick out some of the main issues from the essay and address these in a summative manner. Your tutor will want to see that you have been able to reach a conclusion and that in concluding you are able to use the appropriate areas from within your study. This section will also demonstrate how you can disseminate your findings, say what you are going to do with this new knowledge that you now have. One model for the conclusion is that it is a mirror image of the introduction in that the first few sentences are focused on the actual contents of the essay, followed by the final sentences that apply to a wider area, as illustrated in Figure 3.4.

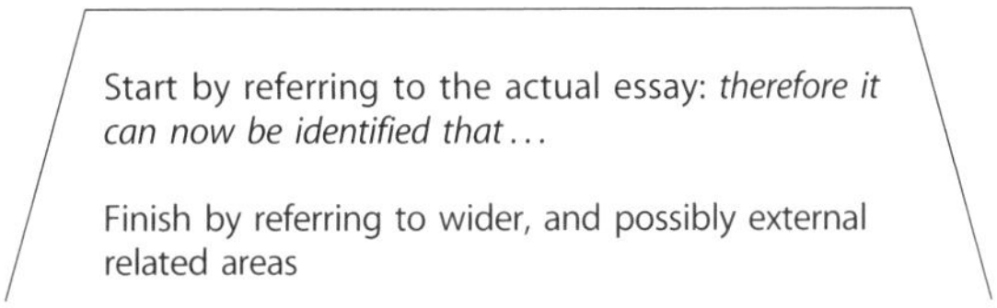

Start by referring to the actual essay: *therefore it can now be identified that . . .*

Finish by referring to wider, and possibly external related areas

Figure 3.4 Conclusion model (The reverse of the Introduction)

Case Study

Jenny had completed her initial teacher training two years ago by achieving a BA(Hons) with qualified teacher status in primary teaching. She obtained a post teaching Key Stage 2 at a large primary school on the outskirts of a city. Jenny found her first year difficult: addressing all the standards took effort and time and Jenny struggled to juggle all her responsibilities. When the CPD co-ordinator at the school asked Jenny to consider taking part in the MTL as part of her CPD, her initial response was to opt not to engage with the master's degree, as the memories of her first year in teaching were still fresh in her mind and served to undermine her confidence in her own ability to study. Jenny was offered help with study skills and academic writing and immediately began to feel more confident about her development. She has registered for a master's degree and is completing the third module, after having successfully completed the first two. Jenny has reported that lack of confidence and a poor previous experience, as well as a busy teaching job and young family had initially given her the excuse not to engage with master's-level CPD.

Referencing

Referencing is the recording of your reading. As discussed in the previous chapter, you need to develop a process whereby you record your reading. As a rule of thumb, when recording your reading you need to offer sufficient information so that the reader can find the texts for themselves. There are several referencing systems, all of which provide the reader with the relevant information albeit in a slightly different manner. For the purpose of this study guide, the Harvard system will be described and used throughout the book. In other words, referencing, or citing as it is sometimes called, is taking information from something you have read and placing this in your own work to either support or contradict your discussion and analysis. Whenever you use information that is from another work you must reference the source in your own text and in the reference list or bibliography. Obtaining information from other sources widens your perspective and demonstrates that you can access a variety of texts. For the MTL, you will need to demonstrate that you can obtain text from different sources, for instance books, journals and websites.

Referencing correctly helps you to avoid plagiarism, which is using ideas or words from someone else and passing them off as your own. It is a very serious offence and will, without exception, incur severe penalties. There are three main methods of referencing.

- *Direct quotation* is where you copy text word-for-word, from an article. It is considered good academic practice, when quoting to use short quotes to support your work. In your text you need to enclose it in quotation marks and reference your source, including the page number. See the examples in Table 3.3.
- *Paraphrasing* is when you read and understand the meaning of text from a source, and express it in your own words within your text. You will have used ideas and general themes from this source, so you must therefore reference it appropriately. For this reference, you do not need to use quotation marks, nor do you need the page number.
- *Summarising* is where you read and understand text from another source, and briefly refer to the main idea within your own text.

Secondary referencing

If you want to use a piece of information from one author who is cited in another author's work, reference it as follows:

Orden (cited in Henderson, 2000, p2) describes how teachers need to 'deconstruct the curriculum'. By this, she is referring to the ability to understand and learn new skills.

It could be argued that teachers need to 'deconstruct the curriculum'. This means that in order to understand and learn new skills, a teacher needs to apply them to their own practice (Orden, cited in Vella, 2001, p42).

Electronic referencing

Refer in the text in the same way as for a book or journal; however do not put the website address for any electronic sources in the assignment text – this will go in your bibliography.

Drinkwater, P. (2001) Portfolios for assessment: *Educational Management Series*. London: Routledge. **www.netLibrary.com** [accessed 03 April 2000].

Reference list or bibliography?

A reference list is the alphabetical (by author's surname) list that follows the essay which is the record of all the texts directly referred to in the writing. A bibliography is the alphabetical list that follows the essay which is the record of all the texts that have been used in order to develop knowledge about the essay subject, but have not necessarily been directly referred to in the text. For example, you might access several books or journals to help you to understand a particular area of the MTL but you may not wish to refer directly to any of these.

Table 3.3 Referencing in text

Quoting direct text from a book:	Referencing the quote:
Role play is important when encouraging students to develop as it 'encourages reflection and enables students to experience another role' (Corton, 2002, p8)	Corton, T. (2002) *Role play in professional development*. London: Sage
Or include the author's name as part of your sentence: this helps the sentence to flow. For example:	
According to Corton (2002, p8) role play 'encourages reflection and enables students to experience another role'	
Quoting text from a journal:	Referencing the quote:
'A plethora of terms has been used to describe the various roles of staff directly supporting the learning of pupils in schools, but who are not employed as qualified teachers' (Rhodes, 2006, p158)	Rhodes, C. (2006) The impact of leadership and management on the construction of professional identity in school learning mentors. *Educational studies*, 32 (2), pp157–69
Or when quoting from an article written by several people:	Rhodes, C.P., Nevill, A. and Allen, J. (2004) Valuing and supporting teachers: A survey of satisfaction, dissatisfaction, morale and retention in an English local education authority. *Research in Education*, 71 (3), pp67–80
'The supply and retention of teachers continues to present challenges for the UK government in its drive to raise standards and attainment in schools' (Rhodes et al., 2004)	
Summarising from book text:	Referencing the summary:
Douglas has written extensively on the control of knowledge and direction of consensus within an organisation (Douglas, 1992)	Douglas, M. (1992) *Risk and Blame: Essays in cultural theory*. London: Routledge.
Summarising from journal text:	Referencing the summary:
The role of support staff in schools involves supporting teaching staff as well as pupils. (Rhodes, 2006)	Rhodes, C. (2006) The impact of leadership and management in the construction of professional identity in school learning mentors. *Educational Studies*, 32 (2), pp157–69
Paraphrasing from book text:	Referencing the paraphrase:
Cultures use danger as a bargaining tool, each culture uses a different danger in order for that culture to survive and develop (Douglas,1992)	Douglas, M. (1992) *Risk and Blame: Essays in cultural theory*. London: Routledge
Paraphrasing the journal text:	Referencing the paraphrase:
According to Rhodes (2006), the effective management of school support staff is crucial if they are to support teachers and pupils in an appropriate manner	Rhodes, C. (2206) The impact of leadership and management in the construction of professional identity in school learning mentors. *Educational Studies*, 32 (2), pp157–69

Summary

This chapter has addressed many of the key areas surrounding the development of writing at a level appropriate to the MTL. It has focused on areas such as:

- identifying an appropriate topic;
- planning and developing the essay;
- key terms used in assessment criteria;
- managing literature;
- referencing.

References and **Further reading**

Blaxter, L., Hughes, C. and Tight, M. (1996) *How to research*. Buckingham: Open University Press.

Campbell, A., McNamara, O. and Gilroy, P. (2004) *Practitioner Research and Professional Development in Education*. London: Paul Chapman Publishing.

King, S. (2000) *On Writing, a Memoir of the Craft*. London: Hodder & Stoughton.

Murray, R. (2002) *How to Write a Thesis* (2nd edn). Maidenhead: Open University Press/McGraw-Hill.

Murray, R. and Moore, S. (2006) *The Handbook of Academic writing: A fresh approach*. Maidenhead: Open University Press/McGraw-Hill.

Schön, D. (1991) *The Reflective Practitioner: How professionals think in action*. Aldershot: Arena.

Silverman, D. (2000) *Doing Qualitative Research: A practical handbook*. London: Sage.

CHAPTER 4

Introduction to research

Chapter Objectives

This chapter will identify what research is and how it can be used in the classroom. It will enable you to discover the fundamentals of research and to reflect on how research could complement your own practice and vice versa. By the end of this chapter, you should be able to:

- develop an understanding of research;
- identify different research paradigms;
- demonstrate an understanding of the way in which a research project is carried out;
- identify an appropriate area for research within your own practice.

Links to standards
This chapter will help you to address the following professional teaching standards.

C3 Maintain an up-to-date knowledge and understanding of the professional duties of teachers and the statutory framework within which they work, and contribute to the development, implementation and evaluation of the policies and practice of your workplace, including those designed to promote equality of opportunity.

C6 Have a commitment to collaboration and co-operative working where appropriate.

C7 Evaluate your performance and be committed to improving your practice through appropriate professional development.

C8 Have a creative and constructively critical approach towards innovation; being prepared to adapt your practice where benefits and improvements are identified.

C10 Have a good up-to-date working knowledge and understanding of a range of teaching, learning and behaviour management strategies and know how to use and adapt them, including how to personalise learning to provide opportunities for all learners to achieve their potential.

C15 Have a secure knowledge and understanding of your subjects/curriculum areas and related pedagogy including: the contribution that your subjects/curriculum areas can make to cross-curricular learning; and recent relevant developments.

C17 Know how to use skills in literacy, numeracy and ICT to support your teaching and wider professional activities.

P2 Have an extensive knowledge and understanding of how to use and adapt a range of teaching, learning and behaviour management strategies, including how to personalise learning to provide opportunities for all learners to achieve their potential.

Introduction

In the previous two chapters you were asked to think about and develop higher-level study and academic writing skills; this chapter will offer you the opportunity to apply these skills to the area of research. Murray and Moore (2006, p159) found that academics often view research and teaching to be a 'constant tension'. This was due to the perceived difficulty in allocating time to writing when the teaching timetable was felt to take most of the teachers' time resource. This tension would seem to emanate from the teachers' perceptions of research. For example, many teachers view research as something that is fundamentally different from their own practice, yet this does not need to be the case. The MTL is firmly based around the practice area and therefore will enable teachers to use the time spent in the classroom as time spent researching. This chapter will introduce the concept of research and will enable you to begin to identify areas within your own practice that could be developed as a research project. A word of caution is sounded by Boud and Solomon (2001), in that they suggest a gulf separates work-based learning and collaborative research due to the fact that they exist in different conceptual areas. Work-based learning in the area of teaching and learning, and research in the area of innovation and consultancy. This could provide a challenge for universities and for work-based learners; however, if strong work-based research support is available and teachers are guided in the practice of research within their own work area, this gulf could be bridged. The nature of the MTL would support this bridging process in terms of focusing the teachers' learning and research on their own practice. Stenhouse (1975) wrote extensively on teachers as researchers and concluded that a significant amount of work would need to be carried out if teachers are to see themselves as researchers. Later in this chapter some of the barriers to research are explored in more depth.

There are different approaches to the way in which research is conducted and these are discussed in more detail later on. Also, this chapter will identify the reasons for research and how the MTL can help to develop research skills in the classroom, thereby offering you the opportunity to reflect on your own practice in order to identify appropriate potential research projects or areas.

What is this thing called research?

We are faced with the impact of research every day. Research and the results from research projects are transferred into our lives through the media, newspapers, books, journals and television documentaries in the form of reports, accounts and theories. For example, we know that smoking is bad for our health because research has been carried out in this field and the results are consistent with the effects of smoking being detrimental to health. Similarly, we are aware that certain medications successfully treat some medical conditions because of drugs research trials. You can therefore begin to reflect on how some research impacts on you, but before reaching this stage, a cyclical process has been carried out, and it is this that will provide the focus for discussion here. Blaxter et al. (2001) point out that many research skills are easily witnessed in the practice area, for example, the ability to ask questions and listen to answers, the ability to make notes and to consider the notes that have been made. You will carry out small research tasks every day, probably without realising that is what you are doing. A useful and straightforward definition of research has been offered by Bassey (1999, p38) as a *systematic, critical and self-critical enquiry which aims to contribute towards the advancement of knowledge and wisdom*. To look deeper at this definition, the word 'enquiry' will be further explored. People have been carrying out enquiries into aspects of the environment within which they live for many years. The means by which this is done can be classified in three areas: experience, reasoning, and research (Mouly, 1978). Each of these areas does not operate in isolation, but rather they are mutually complementary (Cohen et al., 2000).

Experience

In an effort to try to understand what is going on, for example, within the classroom, you will use your experience in applying a 'common sense' knowledge to the situation. This method, however, is flawed, as you can only apply what you yourself know and this will depend on your own lived experiences. Your colleagues will have a different set of lived experiences and therefore will apply a different common sense to the same situation. Using your common sense has many limitations; for example, if you carry out an enquiry in an informal, uncritical and haphazard manner, you will probably obtain results that are selective and based on a hunch or subjective view. If, however, a researcher were to carry out a similar enquiry, they would be more likely to use a more critical and systematic approach. They will collect data without bias of belief or value, and construct theories through an objective and organised process that addresses all aspects of the enquiry. An example of this might be the teacher who has identified a behaviour change in one of the pupils following the morning break. If this alteration in behaviour has happened on two or three occasions, the teacher is likely to assume a causal link between the break and the change in behaviour of the pupil. However, a researcher is going to want to execute a structured and rigorous experiment that looks at other reasons or variables why there might be a change in behaviour.

Reasoning

Reasoning takes place in one of two ways: deductive or inductive. Deductive reasoning is how you deduce something through a sequential process of logical consideration, for example: *All banks process money, Floyds CSP is a bank, therefore, Floyds CSP processes money*. Alternatively, inductive reasoning can be explained by starting from a point of no preconceived ideas. Data and evidence are collected and once sufficient has been identified, themes and relationships will be generated from the data. For example, you might suspect that a certain way of working improves pupil attainment. If you wanted to find out more you would start with a reasonably blank canvas, ask questions and read around the subject in order to gain more information. The third method by which we set out to identify the truth is that of research.

Different research approaches

Two main approaches to research exist and they are determined by what it is you want to find out and which view of social science is dominant. Cohen et al. (2000, p5) explained that:

> Education research has ...absorbed two competing views of the social sciences – the established, traditional view and a recent interpretive view. The former holds that the social sciences are essentially the same as the natural sciences and are therefore concerned with discovering natural and universal laws regulating and determining individual and social behaviour; the latter view, however, while sharing the rigour of the natural sciences and the same concern of traditional social science to describe human behaviour, emphasises how people differ from inanimate natural phenomena and from each other.

This means that there are two very different ways of looking at issues of society, the established traditional view, or positivist approach, and the more recent interpretivist view or anti-positivist approach. Research investigations are wholly influenced by the approach that is chosen.

Table 4.1 is a useful summary of the two approaches.

Table 4.1 Positivist and anti-positivist approaches

Positivist approach	Anti-positivist or interpretivist approach
Is deductive	Is inductive
Starts with a theory of how something works and tests, via, for example experiments, if it is true	Starts with a blank canvas and seeks to create a theory from identifying what exists
Focuses on the belief that all truth and knowledge can be obtained by observing or experiencing the real world	Focuses on the belief that truth cannot be claimed by observation or experience alone. Truth can be interpreted through enquiry and interaction with the real world
Often described as scientific	Often described as naturalistic
Offers better control of variables	Less control of variables – research design emerges from the interaction with the study
Structured methodology (discussed in next chapter) mainly leading to statistical analysis	Negotiated outcomes. Meaning is negotiated with the respondents of the research
Example title 1 *A study to identify what percentage of male teachers progress to primary school management*	Example title 1 *Why do men become primary head teachers?*
Example title 2 *No-man's land: Is the ratio of female to male primary school teachers increasing?*	Example title 2 *An investigation into why there are so few men teaching in primary schools*

The positivist approach to research is usually demonstrated by a quantitative methodology and the anti-positivist approach by a qualitative methodology.

Quantitative research is concerned with the collection of numerical or figurative data. It can be analysed in terms of numbers and is based on structured plans. For example, the participants of the research, often called the sample, will be identified and this sample will be stringently adhered to throughout: the researcher will not add any other people or variables to the study. Take for example, the national census. A particular sample of the population is identified and surveyed but there is no facility for the participants to engage in, or record anything other than the basic statistical data that is required on the census form, neither are other groups of people added to the research sample. Punch (2000) offered the view that in order to fully understand the concept of quantitative research, one must appreciate that it is much more than simply collecting and analysing data in terms of numbers; he advocated that when conducting quantitative investigations, the researcher must adapt their way of thinking to enable an approach that involves several methods of data collection. On the other hand, qualitative research is concerned with the collection of data in many forms, for example, interviewing people, entering into discussions, observing group interactions and reviewing documents. It tends to focus on the in-depth exploration of a subject, which often leads to the researcher needing to be spontaneous, and therefore adding extra participants as necessary as the study progresses. The qualitative researcher often involves themselves in the setting that they are researching, allowing the participants to speak for themselves, and in so doing offering their own perspectives and values. Qualitative research is an interactive process that allows both researcher and participant the opportunity to discuss the issues being studied. Silverman (2000) pointed out that qualitative research is a useful research approach when studying people's life histories or the daily behaviour of groups. He further suggested that qualitative researchers favour this method as they believe it can offer a deeper and more detailed view of the particular social phenomena being studied. The table below offers a comparison of the two approaches.

Table 4.2 Quantitative and qualitative research

Quantitative research	Qualitative research
Concerned with data in the form of numbers	Concerned with data in the form of words
Is mostly objective	Is mostly subjective
Surveys the sample using set questions, often with yes–no options for answers. (Other methods can be used and will be discussed in the following chapter)	Interviews the sample using discussion to identify why, how, what, where and when. (Other methods can be used and will be discussed in the following chapter)
Is scientific and structured	Is naturalistic and flexible
Used often in health and medicine; for example, to determine the geographic spread of disease	Used often in social sciences; for example, to determine teachers' perspectives of the introduction of the MTL

Reflective Task

Reflecting on your own practice, identify an opportunity for research. You may wish to consider a particular area that you feel could be improved, or perhaps you might want to develop a new procedure or strategy for the school. Give some thought to how you might find out the information that would help you to carry out your research. Would you use a quantitative or qualitative approach? Also, think about the consequences of your research: which groups could it benefit?

The overall aims of the research – why do we research?

That you are reading about research in a book dedicated to the study skills for MTL, is probably indicative of the likelihood that you are performing research as an exercise to fulfil the criteria for a module within the MTL, or for any investigative element of your study. It is worth considering that teachers will be carrying out research as part of their own practice aside from any CPD activity. Essentially the skills are the same; the difference is in the reporting. As an MTL participant, you will need to satisfy the assessment criteria set out within the degree programme, whereas a teacher carrying out research to support their practice will not need to do this. Research is therefore conducted in order to further knowledge and identify truth in a given area. However, this could also be as part of a CPD programme.

Silverman (2000) drew attention to the point of view that books about research should include details of personal situations if they are to be received as helpful and interesting. Therefore authors of research books need to include material that is suitable, understandable and appropriate, if the student is to benefit from the literature.

The following three scenarios are taken from a recent research investigation carried out for a doctoral thesis. Two demonstrate the research approach of teachers, both of whom were completing their master's degree, the third offers some insight into my own research plan, that of the doctoral thesis.

Case Studies

Judy's dissertation proposal

Judy was a maths teacher in a large secondary school. She was taking part in a master's degree in educational leadership and management as she wanted to progress her career. Judy was interested in comparing the maths success of male pupils at Key Stage 4, with female pupils' success at the same key stage. She wanted to identify if, as she suspected, there was a significant difference in the success rate between boys and girls. For this investigation, given that she was looking at percentages and numbers of pupils succeeding, she followed a quantitative approach. However, once she had identified the percentage, she was in the process of considering whether to further develop the investigation by, in the future, looking into why the difference in success was so marked. With this in mind, her future research approach would probably need to be a qualitative study.

Paul's work-based action research project

Paul is a deputy head in a large rural secondary school. His main interest is the relationship of children's behaviour on learning. He is of the belief that poor behaviour might have something to do with the poor results experienced by several classes within his school. His research focused on two classes, and looked at how the poor behaviour of some of the pupils within each class impacted on the learning and results of the group. He wanted to identify the teachers' views and feelings regarding behaviour, he also wanted to find out what the views of the children were. The views of parents and teaching support staff were also acknowledged. Paul therefore used a qualitative approach to his research.

Karen's thesis plan

I am interested in what influences teachers in their decisions to engage with, or disengage from, continuing professional development, in particular, master's degree-level development. The plan developed around the need for data from teachers who were engaging in CPD, and also from teachers who had withdrawn from CPD programmes. The data needed to reflect teachers' feelings and views, and also the opinion and attitude of head teachers, local authority figures and university tutors involved in delivering master's-level CPD. A qualitative approach was therefore used. Data was collected by interviews, researcher observation and group interviews.

The three short accounts demonstrate the reasons behind the decision to investigate a certain phenomena, as well as the approach that was used. The MTL may require you to carry out a research project. It is worth bearing this in mind from the onset of the master's programme, as you can begin to develop a research plan for the MTL at an early stage. You can begin to address areas of your own practice that you feel are worth further investigation. The question often asked by teachers embarking on a master's degree is: *What sorts of things do teachers research for their studies?* The answer is practically always the same: *any area of their practice that is interesting to them and which warrants further investigation.* You might identify areas that you feel fall short of being effective, you may know that there are problems of some sort within the classroom that could benefit from further study. Similarly, you might be responsible for a particular area of the curriculum, and want to find new and innovative ways of complementing the delivery. It really is a matter for you to decide; however, you are not alone in this. Your tutor will help you to define a focus for your study, but you need to have some ideas initially to take to them in order to discuss.

Barriers to research

After working in the area of teacher CPD for several years, it has become evident that there are many reasons that teachers give as barriers to carrying out research. The following points set out some of these and offer explanations as to why they may be regarded as barriers.

- *Research is time-consuming, and I simply do not have any extra time.* This is one of the most common reasons given for not engaging in research. Teachers are, without doubt, time-pressured, and often have busy lives outside of education; however, there are not many occupations and professions nowadays that enjoy vast amounts of spare or free time. Most public-sector occupations are extremely frenetic and offer little time for anything other than the daily routine. But this is just the point: research can be part of this daily routine. It might seem to be something different, but it is no different to having something else attached to your agenda. For example, your manager may introduce another responsibility to your role within school. The benefit with carrying out research is that you can normally drive the project. If you are the main or sole researcher, the study is yours. You are therefore able to plan what you do, and if you use your own classroom as the research area, you reduce the amount of any travelling and data-collection time. If you are new to teaching, it is probably best to start researching from the very beginning of your career. Use the MTL as your first research project and carry on researching; this way you will always consider it a part of your role.

- *Research is a different language completely – it is a different way of life; I don't have the time to learn a new language.* The issue of time has been discussed in the previous point; however, the view that research is a different language is worthy of further acknowledgement here, as it is a common concern. There are many tensions around how teachers view themselves academically, and also, how they are viewed by others. The view that teachers are not academics has been aired many times by teachers and school managers. These groups argue that when teachers are looked upon as academics by others, this has the impact of creating a perception that teachers are able to engage in high-level academic practice, when actually they consider themselves practical, classroom managers. Conversely, some teachers are quite comfortable with the academic label, and therefore approach higher-level study from a different perspective. My research has revealed that a large number of teachers participating in master's-level study begin by seeing themselves as pragmatic, practical people, who are concerned with the day-to-day classroom delivery of the curriculum, and they seem to view this in opposition to being academic. However, by the end of the programme, many of these teachers begin to change their perceptions of themselves, and start to believe that they are worthy of the title of 'academic'. This point is central to the issue of research being a different language, as once teachers begin to believe in their ability to study and carry out research investigations, they start to relate to the language of research. It is acknowledged that research, like any other discourse, has a set of ideas, values and narrative that is encapsulated within the discipline, and this can be perceived as jargon; however, it is no different to areas such as sport, literature, health, politics, etc., in that the jargon can be learnt and understood. The important thing to take from this point is that the language of research is not just for the sole use of experienced and hardened researchers, it is there to be practised and used by anyone with an interest in the area. Give yourself permission to begin to learn about research.

- *Research is a pointless waste of time and money.* The media are often used as a vehicle to report on certain research studies. Recent research that has been reported in this way has included such things as: *Postnatal depression – in the genes.* (Hill, 2008), *Latitude 4,595N, Longitude 48,085E: We find the hijacked Sirius star* (Jones, 2008), *Soft degrees need less work by students* (Paton, 2008). From these newspaper report headlines, it is apparent that they would probably only appeal to a certain group of the population, those with an interest in the subject, so for other newspaper readers, these reports could serve to act as a demotivating factor when considering carrying out research themselves. The statement that describes research as pointless was given by a teacher who referred to similar newspaper reports and felt that much of what was reported in the media was pointless. Your research will not be pointless – in fact, in order that it satisfies the assessment criteria for the MTL, it will be absolutely appropriate and valuable to your practice. Without the administration of prescribed insulin, the diabetic person would not survive and without research, how would we have known about the effectiveness of insulin? Similarly, it is as a result of research that we have a better understanding of such areas as: healthy diet, the usefulness of exercise, the effectiveness of using car seatbelts to reduce injury in many accidents, and the most effective training routines for Olympic athletes.

   The issue of money and funding for research is dependent on who is carrying out the research and how the findings will be disseminated. For example, small-scale, school-based research may not require a significant amount of funding, if any, and could therefore be funded locally by the head teacher. On the other hand, a large-scale national study into the effectiveness of a particular curriculum issue, carried out by a research consultancy on behalf of the government, would incur heavy financial penalties. The research that you carry out for the MTL is not likely to require a significant amount of money, largely due to the fact that you will carry out your study in your practice area.

- *Research is something that is carried out by researchers and I'm a teacher.* The barrier here is that some teachers see teaching and research as competing tensions. The government view is for all teachers to engage in research within their practice that can help to have a positive impact on the school as a whole (DfEE, 2001). The area of tension would appear to be the question of whether by being a teacher, one can also be a researcher and it would seem that in some cases this is a rather disabling tension. Campbell et al. (2004) put forward the view that by carrying out research, teachers can become empowered and as a result, offer themselves as a voice within the arena of policy development. Conversely, Elliott (1991) points out that encouraging teachers to research does not necessarily provide the opportunity for empowerment, but rather, leads to the teachers feeling that they are taking part in action research in order to justify the government's policy in the acceleration of standards. With whichever argument you concur, the focus of interest is fundamentally the same. The way in which teachers approach research depends on the way in which they view their role as a classroom practitioner, and if, in their view, this involves carrying out research.

Research questions

Your research area will need to have a particular emphasis and will need to address one, or a set of questions. It is these questions that will focus the work and determine the methodology. Below are several example questions; have a look at them and give some thought to what the research is actually trying to find out.

Question 1

- What do school staff think of performance-related pay?
- What do teachers and managers in the three schools of the study think about performance-related pay in terms of (a) their work practice? (b) their relations with colleagues? and (c) their professional identity?
- Performance-related pay is going to raise academic standards in The Briars primary school over the next three years.

Question 2

- What do teachers think about the MTL?
- The MTL will raise pupil success standards in those schools where the majority of staff engage in the master's programme.
- How will the MTL impact on the practice of teachers?

Question 1 is a question regarding performance-related pay but by asking the questions as they are laid out, different aspects will be identified. The last bullet point sets out a hypothesis that the research will test.

Question 2 again asks different things about the same subject, the second bullet point is a hypothesis. the first and third bullet points seem similar, but offer different perspectives.

One of the most common difficulties encountered when carrying out research for the first time, is that new researchers do not clearly define what it is they want to find out. You are advised to give this some careful thought and ask your tutor for advice as necessary. You might need to continually ask yourself what it is that you are trying to learn, what are you attempting to identify? By keeping the research questions at the front of your mind, you are more likely to be able to stick to your focus and not get sidetracked. You may be asked to complete a research proposal, and this will help you to refine your questions and test the area prior to carrying out the main topic.

Case Study

Sumatra Singh is head teacher of Whernside High School. She has been concerned for some time that the current school does not engage with local businesses and employers.

She feels that, in order to build successful relationships in the local community, the school needs to be seen as the provider of the future workforce for the local area. Sumatra wants to form links and partnerships with some of the organisations within the area; however, she realises that this needs to be done sensitively and with care. She has secured agreement from governors to carry out a research investigation that will help to identify the best way to proceed with this initiative. Sumatra has written a questionnaire that she will send to local businesses and she has asked to meet with the manager from a selection of organisations that neighbour the school.

Reflective Task

With regard to the case study above, give some thought to the research questions that Sumatra is likely to use. What does she actually want to find out? What barriers might she experience?

Research proposal

This can either be something that you do informally between you and your tutor, or something that is more formal, and in certain cases assessed as a piece of work in its own right. Whatever format the proposal takes, it is likely to include the following.

Identification of the research topic and aims of the project. You will probably already have an idea of the area that you want to investigate. Be cautious, as many a good idea has been dismissed at this point due to not being thought through appropriately.

Scale of the project. Be sure to identify from the outset that your research topic is manageable. You need to be able to do what you say you are going to do, with the resources that you have. A large-scale project may make this unachievable.

Time. The research proposal is an exercise that allows you to identify a timetable. It will enable you to set a structure to your project from the first interview or meeting to the report writing. Be realistic here: you are more likely to adhere to your timetable if it reflects reality.

Literature review. You will need to have some idea of the literature that you will need to access and you will also need to know if you can access the literature readily. By this stage you will have developed an understanding of the key authors in your field, but be open to the possibility that new authors may have emerged and to any changes in government legislation.

Technology. Give consideration to how you will word-process the documentation that you begin to build, making sure that you save your documents and back up your work. Be paranoid about your electronic files and folders, as once you have pressed the Delete button, without saving, you will lose your work. It is suggested that you save your work to an external source, either a memory stick or similar.

Practical Task

Once you have identified an area for research, make some notes of how you might find out the information that will support your research. This will depend on your chosen research approach. For example, if you want to obtain figurative information from a wide sample, you may wish to send out a questionnaire, in which case you can write down 20 questions that will help you to form an opinion of what it is you want to find out. Alternatively, you may wish to find out what your colleagues' views are about something. Where this is the case, write down some questions that will support your interview.

Summary

This chapter has offered guidance on the basics of research: it has addressed those areas to consider at the start of your research project, but that are of equal importance as the project develops. The MTL will require you to carry out research and this chapter can act as a reference point for you, in particular in terms of the following areas.
- Aims of the research project.
- Different research approaches.
- Considerations when starting a research project.
- Barriers to research.
- Research proposals.

References and **Further reading**

Bassey, M. (1999) *Case Study in Educational Settings*. Buckingham: Open University Press.

Blaxter, L., Hughes, C. and Tight, M. (2001) *How to Research*. Buckingham: Open University Press.

Boud, D. and Solomon, N. (2001) *Work based Learning: A new higher education?* Buckingham: Open University Press.

Campbell, A., McNamara, O. and Gilroy, P. (2004) *Practitioner Research and Professional Development in Education*. London: Paul Chapman Publishing.

Cohen, L., Manion, L. and Morrison, K. (2000) *Research methods in Education* (5th edn) Abingdon: RoutledgeFalmer.

Department for Education and Employment (2001) *Learning and Teaching: A strategy for professional development*. Green Paper. London: DfEE.

Elliott, J. (1991) *Action Research for Educational Change*. Buckingham: Open University Press.

Hill, A. (2008) Post natal depression: in the genes. *The Observer*, 2 November 2008, p18. London: Guardian Newspaper Group.

Jones, S. (2008) Latitude 4.595N, longitude 48.085E: we find the hijacked Sirius star. *The Guardian*, 27 November 2008, p13. London: Guardian Newspaper Group.

Mouly, G.J. (1978) in Cohen, L., Mannion, L. and Morrison, K. (2000) *Research Methods in Education*, (5th edn) Abingdon: RoutledgeFalmer.

Murray, R. and Moore, S. (2006) *The Handbook of Academic Writing: A fresh approach*. Maidenhead: Open University Press/McGraw-Hill.

Paton, G. (2008) Soft degrees need less work by students. *Daily Telegraph*, November 25 2008, p14. London: Telegraph Newspaper Group.

Punch, K. (2000) *Developing Effective Research Proposals*. London: Sage.

Silverman, D. (2000) *Doing Qualitative Research: A practical handbook*. London: Sage.

Stenhouse, L. (1975) *An Introduction to Curriculum Research and Development*. Oxford: Heinemann.

CHAPTER 5

Research methodologies

Chapter Objectives

By the end of this chapter, you should be able to:
- develop an understanding of what is meant by research methodology;
- analyse different research methodologies;
- critically reflect on key issues relating to methodologies, including validity and reliability;
- demonstrate an understanding of the way in which your own practice area could support a research project.

Links to standards

This chapter will help you to address the following professional teaching standards.

C2 Hold positive values and attitudes and adopt high standards of behaviour in your professional role.

C3 Maintain an up-to-date knowledge and understanding of the professional duties of teachers and the statutory framework within which they work, and contribute to the development, implementation and evaluation of the policies and practice of your workplace, including those designed to promote equality of opportunity.

C7 Evaluate your performance and be committed to improving your practice through appropriate professional development.

C10 Have a good up-to-date working knowledge and understanding of a range of teaching, learning and behaviour management strategies and know how to use and adapt them, including how to personalise learning to provide opportunities for all learners to achieve their potential.

P2 Have an extensive knowledge and understanding of how to use and adapt a range of teaching, learning and behaviour management strategies, including how to personalise learning to provide opportunities for all learners to achieve their potential.

P5 Have a more developed knowledge and understanding of your subjects/curriculum areas and related pedagogy including how learning progresses within yourself.

P10 Contribute to the professional development of colleagues through coaching and mentoring, demonstrating effective practice, and providing advice and feedback.

E1 Be willing to take a leading role in developing workplace policies and practice and in promoting collective responsibility for their implementation.

E2   Research and evaluate innovative curricular practices and draw on research outcomes and other sources of external evidence to inform your own practice and that of colleagues.

E14 Contribute to the professional development of colleagues using a broad range of techniques and skills appropriate to your needs so that you demonstrate enhanced and effective practice.

Introduction

This chapter will focus on the practice of carrying out a research project; it will aim to inform you of some of the research strategies in a manner that is jargon-free and accessible. The chapter will attempt to demystify some of the issues surrounding research and in so doing will identify the skills and techniques involved in carrying out a research project. The MTL will require you to carry out at least one small-scale research investigation, and it is hoped that the information contained within this and the previous chapter will offer some guidance and direction to support your learning. Let us assume that you have identified some area of your practice that is confusing or challenging you. You have noticed that a certain resource or teaching aid that is supposed to encourage learning, is not apparently effective with several of the pupils. Similarly, you may have read something in the press or heard something on the media that could affect what you do in the classroom. If you have stopped for a moment to consider how these things might influence your work or the way in which your pupils learn, you have taken the first steps to becoming a researcher as you have identified an area that is worthy of investigation. This chapter will take this a stage further and will address the methods and techniques used in order to become a researcher and carry out an investigation at a level that is appropriate to the MTL.

What do we mean by methodology?

'Methodology' is the name given to the process of studying a certain phenomenon. It has been described by Silverman (2000, p88) as *a general approach to studying research topics … shaping which methods are used and how each method is used*. From this statement it can be identified that methodology and methods are two different, albeit related, processes. A common misunderstanding experienced by teachers new to research is the difference between methodology and method. Before you progress through this chapter, please take some time to understand these two areas. The methods you use form part of the methodology – put another way, the methodology you choose will influence the types of methods you execute to collect the data. The methodology is the overarching term which encompasses what you do in order to carry out your investigation. Table 5.1 shows the relationship between methodology and method.

Table 5.1 Methodology and method

	Methodology	Methodology
Method	*Quantitative research*	*Qualitative research*
Observation	Preliminary work, i.e. prior to developing questionnaire	Fundamental to understanding another culture. Used throughout the data collection process of the investigation
Textual analysis	Content analysis, i.e. counting in terms of researchers' categories	Understanding participants' categories
Interviews	Survey research, mainly fixed-choice questions to random samples	Open-ended questions to small samples
Transcripts	Used to check the accuracy of interview records	Used to understand how participants organise their language and communication

(Adapted from Silverman, 2000, p89)

The methodological processes in Table 5.1 are set out as quantitative and qualitative research approaches. These were discussed in detail in Chapter 4 of this book, but it is useful to appreciate that quantitative and qualitative research influence and impact on the methodology used within the investigation. The various research methods can be used for either quantitative or qualitative investigations; however, the way in which they are used will differ, depending on the approach used. Silverman (2000) further suggests that methods should be viewed as research techniques which take on a different meaning according to the methodology used.

Methods

The way in which data is gathered varies depending on which methods are used. Strauss and Corbin (1998, p3) have defined methods as *a set of procedures and techniques for gathering and analyzing data*. It is worth mentioning at this point that there is a vast amount of literature regarding research methods. You are advised to access some of this literature, in particular the titles listed in the further reading section at the end of this chapter, as the focus of this book is reserved for those research methods likely to be useful to your MTL.

Questionnaires

Questionnaires are one of the most widely used research techniques within the field of social research (Blaxter et al., 1996). Devising a set of questions that are then disseminated to a sample of research respondents in order that you receive clear responses to a given phenomena, seems to be straightforward and relatively pain-free. This is not always the case; in fact in very many situations, being able to compose a set of questions for a questionnaire that promotes a response that fully answers your queries can be very difficult and challenging. Bell (2002, p159) concurs with this in her assessment of questionnaires: she believes that they appear to be an easy way to obtain masses of information very quickly, but, she states that they can be *fiendishly difficult*. If you choose questionnaires as a method, you will need to ensure that the questions you pose are clear and unambiguous, and you will need to seek guidance and support, certainly in the initial stages of your questionnaire design, from your mentor, coach or tutor. You need to be able to compose questions that are precise and non-leading, that neither assume nor presume. When designing your questionnaire, you need to decide how you are going to ask the questions.

Give some consideration to the data you are likely to receive from questions asked in the following ways.

1. When did you apply for the MTL?...
2. Why did you apply for the MTL?...
3. Are you engaged in any CPD that relates to the MTL? Yes...(currently)...Yes (previously)...No (never)...
4. How would you describe your head teacher's views in terms of supporting teachers to complete the MTL? a) very positive. b) positive. c) mixed. d) negative. e) very negative.

(It is worth mentioning at this point that if you offer the participants five choices with a neutral selection in the middle, you are offering them the opportunity to remain neutral, when you may need them to make a judgement on either side.)

5. Do you view the MTL as a positive innovation? Yes...No...
6. What do you view as the main advantages of the MTL? Please rank your answers from 1 (most important) to 5 (least important). Positive impact on pupil learning...Increase in self-esteem of teachers...Higher professional status for teaching...Well-qualified and knowledgeable teachers...compare favourably to other professions...
7. Please tell me in your own words what the MTL means to you...

As you can see from the examples of questions posed here, there are many ways of asking similar questions; however, these pose challenges for the way in which you manage the data when you received the questionnaires. Table 5.2 lists some of the benefits and limitations of questionnaires.

Interviews

Generally interviews can be structured, unstructured or semi-structured. If you choose interviews as one of your methods, you will need to decide how structured you want the interview process to be. As a rule of thumb, the more structured the process is, the less opportunity for the participant to be able to speak freely, as you will have a set of questions or themes that you want to pursue. The less structured interview therefore, allows for a high level of free speech and is less focused. It is accepted that all interviews will be taped; this is to enable the interviewer to concentrate on the interview and in guiding the discussion where necessary. You will need to obtain consent to use the tape from the person with whom you are conducting the interview. You may also wish to take notes to support the tape and to clarify any points made by the respondent. Interviews allow for the interviewer

Table 5.2 Questionnaire benefits and limitations

Benefits	Limitations
Question high numbers of people with little outlay of time on your behalf	You can only receive answers to the questions you pose – there is no room for you to further question respondents on their answers
Reasonably inexpensive	Respondents are unable to question the researcher if there are questions that they do not understand
There are different ways in which they can be administered, i.e. posted to respondent's address, over the telephone, via email	Face-to-face questionnaires are time-consuming. Postal questionnaires are likely to have a lower response rate
Respondents may feel that they are less threatening or intimidating than interviews. They can complete them in their own time, own home, etc.	They rely on the self-motivation of the respondent to complete the questionnaire and return the findings to you

to pursue points raised during the discussion, and if the interview is conducted in an appropriate location, where the respondents feel comfortable and relaxed or at ease, you are more likely to engage your participants. Confidentiality and security of information must be considered when selecting an interview venue. Be aware that the participant is going to want to be sure that the information they divulge to you is kept securely and you offer total confidentiality. The structured or semi-structured interview should have as its focus the research questions. This will help you when interpreting the data. An unstructured interview could be challenging when it comes to managing the data, as you may not have a category or section within which you can attribute the information you have received from the interview. When you carry out the interview you need to be able to form a rapport with the respondent, however, you would need to be cautious of appearing too friendly. This could have the effect of the respondent feeling that he or she needs to say whatever pleases you. The first words that you say, accompanied by your facial expressions and body language, will be interpreted by the respondent, and they are likely to make an assessment of you before you have begun to discuss the interview questions. Start off with the easier questions, and allow the participant time to settle into the interview. Remember at all times, the participants are doing you a favour: they will offer you the information you need, providing you have prepared and planned the interview appropriately. Table 5.3 lists some of the benefits and limitations of interviews.

Table 5.3 Interviews benefits and limitations

Benefits	Limitations
Enables flexibility when discussing the research questions – allows researcher to delve deeper where necessary	Interviewing is more likely to offer a smaller participant group than questionnaires
Participants can ask the researcher questions on any ambiguous areas	Depend on the availability of the interviewer and the participant
Interviewer retains all the data. At no time does the participant hold any data	Can become expensive if interviewer has to travel widely to attend interviews with participants in their own area
More than one person could be interviewed at one time	Can be time-consuming for the interviewer

Observations

Observations are not dependent on the respondents' own views or interpretations of the research questions, but rather rely on gathering evidence through the eyes and ears of the researcher, in capturing live data from real events. Cohen et al. (2000, p305) argued that observations, being less predictable than other methods, enable a certain 'freshness' to this form of data collection that is not witnessed by other methods. The researcher is placed within the area and practice of those being investigated, providing the opportunity for the researcher to develop an understanding of the area first hand. Interactions can be witnessed and real practice activities can also be observed, thus enabling the researcher to record critical incidents, which may be overlooked in interviews or questionnaires. The interviewer can participate in the observation in differing degrees, for example, total participation, where the researcher takes on an insider role, or alternatively, as a sideline observer, watching and listening at a distance and not becoming involved with the practice. Insider and outsider researchers are described in more detail later in this chapter. Cohen et al. (2000, p316) sound a note of caution with regard to observation. They warn that observation is not a *morally neutral* practice: observers need to adhere to the same research ethical guidelines as other researchers. If you choose to carry out observations as part of your research on the MTL, you will need to discuss your plans with your mentor, coach or tutor as there are issues of validity and reliability that you will need to address to avoid researcher bias and data contamination.

You will need to maintain clear and robust records that are kept confidentially. Give consideration to the events that you will observe: is there are time relevance? Will you be directed as to which situations you can witness, or will you have some degree of say in where and who you will observe? You will probably need to seek the consent of the head teacher, who may, in turn, need to inform Governors, so you with therefore need to allow time for this process to take place. Table 5.4 lists some of the benefits and limitations of observation.

Table 5.4 Observation benefits and limitations

Benefits	Limitations
Allows the researcher to observe the participants in their own settings	Relies on the researcher's own interpretations of what is taking place
Enables critical incidents to be recorded	Proves challenging for the researcher in terms of having to write copious notes while at the same time observing the practice taking place
Could be less threatening or intimidating than interviews	Participants could change the way in which they act due to the presence of the researcher
No time requirements on behalf of the participants	Time-consuming of behalf of the researcher
Enables the head teacher, management and other colleagues to feel part of the investigation	Gathering data on sensitive or contentious issues could be compromised if participants feel managers are able to witness practice or conversations
Offers the opportunity to obtain a large amount of data in a relatively short space of time	Data has the potential to be disorganised and unstructured

Document analysis

Documents that are likely to provide appropriate information for the MTL include policy documents, rules and regulations, official statistics, inspection reports, curriculum documents, government papers, minutes and agendas of meetings, etc. Analysing documents is akin to critically analysing literature, which has been discussed in a previous chapter. However, there are some subtle yet significant differences when analysing documents. Blaxter et al. (1996, p187) raised the following issues in documentary analysis. They argue that prior to analysing any document for the purposes of research, the following questions must be addressed.

* Who is the author?
* What is the author's position?
* What are their biases?
* Where and when was the document produced?
* Why was the document produced?
* How was it produced and for whom?
* In what context was the document produced?
* What are its underlying assumptions?
* What does the document say, and what does it not say?
* How is the argument presented?
* How well supported and convincing is its argument?
* How does this document relate to previous ones?

- How does this document relate to later ones?
- What do other sources have to day about this document?

Documents should not be read in isolation, as they rarely hold meaning without being compared with other documents or legislation. Cortazzi (2002, p202) argued that in order to analyse documents appropriately, the researcher needs to identify the relation of the document to the social context. Table 5.5. lists some of the benefits and limitations of document analysis.

Table 5.5 Document analysis benefits and limitations

Benefits	Limitations
Allows for a comparison of official information	Can be time-consuming for the researcher
Can be done by the researcher without the involvement of another party	Access to certain documents may be challenging
Can complement other literature or data gathered empirically	Requires secure storage facility for any documents retained by the researcher

Focus groups

This method of gathering data has grown in popularity in social science research. It is primarily a way of collecting qualitative data from a selected group of people, brought together for the purpose of discussing a topic supplied by the researcher. The researcher will be as interested in the interaction between the group as they will the actual responses given to the questions or prompts. Morgan (1988) identified that the following issues need to be addressed when running focus groups.

- Selecting an appropriate number of focus groups to hold on one particular topic, and in so doing, identifying how many people would make up each group.
- Ensuring the participants will be able to take part and have something to offer.
- The researcher needs to be able to offer a steer and guidance within the focus group, at an appropriate level so as to enable a balance between objectivity and disorganised conversation.

The researcher or facilitator needs to take great care in not asking direct questions of one or maybe two people, but rather should guide the discussion and encourage each of the group members to take an active part in the discussion, paying particular attention to the quieter members of the group. Their views are just as important as the participants who like their voice to be heard above others. The researcher will need to record what is said in some way; it is suggested that the focus groups are taped to enable the researcher to concentrate on supporting and facilitating the group. Written notes may need to be taken, but where there are several people interacting at the same time, it would be extremely difficult to capture all of what is said and the way in which it is said, without some form of tape-recording, in particular due to the fact that it is this interaction between group members that is such valuable data that only focus groups can render. The practicalities of organising a focus group involve planning and preparing a suitable room for the group, one in which confidentiality and security can be assured. The researcher will need to decide the focus for discussion and be aware of potential areas for veering off the main topic. Table 5.6. lists some of the benefits and limitations of focus groups.

Table 5.6 Focus groups benefits and limitations

Benefits	Limitations
Allow for the collection of data reasonably quickly from several participants	Some participants may feel that they cannot divulge certain things in the company of colleagues. (This point is contradicted by Frith, 2000)
They can be less intimidating and more spontaneous than interviews, in that interaction within the group can promote humour, etc.	Appropriate space will be needed in which to conduct the focus group
The interaction within the group can promote an area for the responses to be built upon, thereby enabling a progression of argument or discussion	The views of quieter members of the group may be overlooked
Relatively less time-consuming for the participants	Can be time-consuming for the researcher

In considering which methods to use in order to obtain the data that the researcher requires, the research approach needs to be factored in to the methodology. This will also influence the methods and the shape of the research investigation. There are several research approaches. This book will concentrate on the approaches most likely to be used by teachers working towards the MTL and therefore appropriate to use in the classroom or concerning wider school issues.

Action research

Action research is a popular approach among educational researchers. Elliot (1991) defines action research as a cycle that incorporates action-reflection within a professional development systems thinking process. This process, he argues, underpins the qualitative change-management practice that a teacher may explore with their curriculum. The main distinguishing factor that separates action research from other approaches is that it is a study that focuses on the improvement of a social situation. Hart and Bond (1995, p37) set out the following principles of action research.

- Action research is educative.
- It looks upon individuals as being a member of a social group.

- It focuses on a problem and identifies how to improve the problem.
- It is concerned with the future.
- Action research is dependent on a relationship in which those people carrying out the investigation are participants in a change process.

Action research differs from the usual routine practice of the teacher, in that it is a systematic collection of evidence on which critical reflection and analysis can be based. As Elliot (1991, p49) asserts, *the fundamental aim of action research is to improve practice rather than to produce knowledge*. It is not research that is carried out on others, it is a cyclical process that is carried out by a particular researcher to investigate issues from their own work practice, with the aim of improving some aspect of that practice. By studying elements of teaching practice that warrant improvement, you could broaden and deepen your understanding of teaching within the social world. Owing to the fact that action research is concerned with improving practice, a by-product of this improvement process is the implementation of change. Action research could therefore be responsible for change and innovation to the practice area. The process is not complete however, until the consequences of the change have been fully appreciated and learnt by all people concerned. That action research is concerned with improvement and change, implies a political aspect to this research approach.

Kurt Lewin is considered the founder of action research. He suggested that it begins with a general idea of a problem or situation that could benefit from improvement, from which a plan of action can be identified. This plan then leads to a continuing spiral process of data collection, evaluation and analysis, further reconnaissance leading to reconsidering the problem, only to begin the cycle again. Methods used in action research are likely to include questionnaires, interviews, focus groups, observations, examination of field notes and document analysis, as well as literature analysis. At its most effective, action research can result in the empowerment of teachers and teaching, leading to an enhanced professional status and identity. As you work through the MTL, you are likely to identify areas of practice that you feel could be improved, particularly as you become more analytical and critical. Before embarking on an action research investigation, chat to your tutor, coach or mentor, who will help you to refine your research topic and to establish a set of research questions. You will then be able to develop a framework for your study, and, in so doing, identify your methodology.

Practical Task

Have a look at a research article in one of the education journals. Try to identify the approach and methodology used in the article. Find out what the research questions are (these might not be immediately obvious), and critically analyse the article. Then try to have a look at a research article in a health journal (e.g. *Nursing Times*) and again critically analyse this article. Compare the two research designs and data collection.

Case studies

Case study is generally a form of qualitative research, which often uses a mixture of methods, for example, personal observation, interviewing, document analysis, etc. The principal feature of the case study is that it tends to focus on just one example. This could be the researcher's own workplace. Similarly, the focus could be on one individual or on a single group of people. The following list identifies what Bassey has defined as a *useful prescriptive account of what constitutes a worthwhile educational case study.*

An educational case study is an empirical enquiry which is conducted:

- within a localised boundary of space and time;
- into interesting aspects of an educational activity, or programme, or institution, or system;
- mainly in its natural context and within an ethic of respect for persons;
- in order to inform the judgements and decisions of practitioners or policymakers;
- allowing for sufficient data to be collected for the researcher to be able to:
  - explore significant features of the case
  - create plausible interpretations of what is found
  - test the trustworthiness of these interpretations
  - construct a worthwhile argument or story
  - relate an argument or story to relevant research literature
  - convey, in a convincing manner, this argument or story
  - provide an audit trail by which other researchers may validate or challenge the findings.

(Bassey, 2002, p108)

A case study is included within each chapter of this book, and as you will see, it demonstrates the details of a particular case in question. It focuses on a particular location within a defined period of time. And so it is with case study research: the sample is confined to a particular location within a certain timescale. The case study approach is not intended to change practice or initiate innovation, neither is it designed to identify areas of practice that are poor in order to introduce improvements. Its strength is in its ability to detail a particular situation and offer evidence of how the investigation into that particular situation has occurred. If someone reading the case study then compares this to their own practice, and in doing so, recognises areas for research, the case study could have the effect of acting as the catalyst to others' research projects.

Case Study

Marcus has been teaching drama in a secondary school for four years. He has taken part in a CPD programme that has afforded him 120 credits towards a master's degree, and he now wants to complete his degree and therefore has started to prepare for his dissertation. He has worked with his mentor and tutor in deciding on an appropriate subject for his research. He has chosen to look at the use of ICT in drama as his research area. The scope for this is quite large, so he has focused on two main areas: health and safety and the use of stage lighting software. Marcus has identified that there are issues with regard to health and safety in terms of students climbing on step ladders to manage scenery and lighting, he has also discovered that new lighting software can improve the lighting effects on stage. Currently, the lights used are quite old and do not offer support to the scenes as he would like. He feels that the pupils would get a better standard of drama teaching if there were a better lighting system.

Reflective Task

With regard to the case study, reflect on what research approach Marcus would be able to use for his dissertation. What methods would be appropriate? If Marcus were to use a questionnaire, what questions might he ask? What documents or official reports could Marcus access to assist him with his research?

Ethnography

In ethnographic research, the researcher involves themselves within the world that they are investigating. An ethnographic researcher is interested in people and how they make sense of the world that they are in, how they interpret their world and how they interact with others in the same world. This approach to research offers the possibility for the researcher to be a participant observer either covertly or overtly observing people in their situations, normally for an extended period of time. This approach requires the researcher to watch what is happening, listen to conversations, ask questions and collect whatever other data is appropriate and available. An example of ethnography would be the undercover reporter who attempts to identify poor practice in a care home or hospital. Television stations often show programmes in which the reporter is a participant researcher, working within the environment that they are studying in order to try to find out what is going wrong in the area.

Ethnography and anthropology are very similar approaches in that they are both concerned with observing people in a particular setting. Ethnographers and anthropologists both argue that in order to fully understand a group of people one needs to engage with the group for an extended period of time. Ethnography is suited to educational research, particularly where the researcher is a teacher studying issues within the classroom over a lengthy period of time, for example a whole academic year. Imagine a situation where you have identified an area within your practice that you would like to study. Say for example, you want to investigate the effectiveness of a new innovation to a particular key stage. By observing the behaviour of the children within the specific key stage over an academic year, you will be able to identify how they have interacted with each other, how they have

reacted to the innovation and the impact it has had on the group as a whole. This is ethnography, and probably occurring in classrooms around the country every day, yet how many teachers taking part in such research would refer to themselves as ethnographers?
Benefits of ethnographic research include the following.

- If the researcher carries out the ethnography within their workplace, this approach can be less time-consuming for the researcher.
- The researcher is able to observe how the participants interact with each other in the culture that is being researched.
- Ethnography can be relatively inexpensive.
- Mixed methods can be used to support the observations.
- If the researcher is a participant in the process, the research participants are less likely to find the presence of the researcher intimidating.

Limitations to ethnographic research are as follows.

- The observation data relies on the researcher's interpretations.
- If the researcher is a participant in the process, it may be difficult to eliminate bias.
- The researcher must maintain clear and robust field notes and, ideally, a reflective diary or similar.
- A great volume of data is generated. The researcher will need to organise the data in a manner that supports them when attempting to interpret the data.
- Data interpretation can be time-consuming.

Data management, collection and storage

The data is everything when researching. Without the data, the researcher cannot identify with the investigation in any way. When you begin to carry out your research project, make sure that you plan for the data collection and secure storage from the beginning. Remember that you are likely to begin to analyse your data before you complete the data collection. Analysing the data is an ongoing process. Research is a rather disorganised and messy process as it is difficult to maintain a clear and organised stage of events.

Collecting the data

Data collection will occur in many ways, depending on the research approach and methods used. Interview data for example, is likely to be kept on a tape recorder and in notes made by the researcher. Questionnaires will be returned, hopefully in the same format that they were distributed, with the answers to the questions completed. Observation notes will be kept in a research diary or something similar. Focus group data will be stored on a tape recorder and in notes made by the researcher at the time of the focus group. Documents and other necessary literature will be either stored electronically or as a paper file. It is therefore likely that the researcher will accumulate a large amount of data of different appearance. The question is, how can this be managed in a way that makes it reasonably easy to work with? One person's messy and apparently disorganised chaos may be another's order. When you are researching, the key is to find a system that works for you, no matter how disorganised it may appear to others. The important thing is that you can find your way around the data in order to select the particular information that you need. However the data is collected, it is imperative that it is stored securely as the information was given to the researcher for the purpose of the investigation and therefore is regarded as confidential to the researcher.

Analysing the data

Data analysis can take place anytime from when you begin to collect the data: some researchers advocate that, due to the vast amount of data collected, it is useful to begin to analyse the data as soon as possible after it is collected; this method also helps to reduce the chance for the researcher to lose the momentum from the point of collection. When analysing the data for investigations that you have completed for the MTL, it is probably safe to assume that you will analyse some data as you are going along, and once the final piece of data has been collected, spend some time in analysing the sum of the data at the end. You will need to give some consideration to how you will analyse the data: are you, for example, likely to have a long period of time in which you can sit down somewhere quiet to perform your analysis? Or, are you more likely to have to do it in shorter bursts of time, fitting around your teaching schedule? Quantitative data is likely to be made up of measurements, statistics, categories and numbers, for example, and therefore will require sorting and organising in a manner that supports the coding of figurative data. Quantitative data is usually the beginning of the analysis, as once you have the quantitative data, you can do other things with it, you can calculate percentages or averages or values. You can also feed the quantitative data into a qualitative study. The way in which you present the quantitative data will differ from qualitative presentation in that it generally involves a graph, or chart or some sort of image, as opposed to a word document. When analysing quantitative data, you will ask yourself *What do these figures mean?* Similarly, when analysing qualitative data, you will ask *What do these words mean?* This is the first step in interpreting and analysing the information. From your data you will identify a general idea about a particular issue or subject; these ideas are often termed 'concepts'. You may seek to explain this concept, in which case you will refer to 'theory'.

When interpreting and analysing data, it may be necessary to establish themes and codes in order to categorise your data and enable you to manage the analysis in a structured way. You will, for example, analyse taped data in a different manner to field notes for example. When listening to the tape, you will identify that the way in which something is said is very often as important as what is actually said, and you will therefore need to make notes of this on your data notes or transcriptions. Different researchers will interpret data in different ways: two different researchers could be given the same research data and come up with different interpretations. This depends on their own role and position, their own life experiences and knowledge. Some useful issues to be considered when analysing your data for the MTL are summarised as follows.

- Interviews: Is your aim to describe the gritty reality of people's lives or to assess the stories of narratives through which people describe their worlds?
- Field notes: You need to note what you can see (as well as hear) as well as how you are behaving and being treated.
- Texts: Is your goal precise content analysis, in which you establish a set of categories and then count the number of instances that fall into each category? Or is your aim to understand the participants' categories and to see how these are used in concrete activities like telling stories, assembling files or describing family life?
- Transcripts: The preparation of a transcript from an audiotape or a videotape is a theoretically saturated activity. Where there is more than one researcher, sorting out what you are seeing and hearing, it is not just about collating data: it is data analysis.

(Silverman, 2000, pp135–6)

Validity and reliability

Validity is concerned with whether your methodology, methods and technique are appropriate to what it is you want to find out. Hammersley (1990, p57) has defined validity as: *truth, interpreted as the extent to which an account accurately represents the social phenomena to which it refers*. Validity is therefore another word for truth (Silverman, 2000). With regard to the MTL, your tutor, coach or mentor will be able to support you through your search for validity of your work. This support will involve such practice as selecting the current number of variables, deciding which information to leave out and which to include in your research, and keeping the original form in which the data was collected, so that it can be re-examined if necessary. Validity is also to do with how the research data is interpreted, given that the aim of research is to identify how a particular area of the social world works; it is necessary to ensure that the researcher has interpreted the data in an appropriate manner, that the interpretations reflect what is actually going on within the group that is being studied.

Reliability is concerned with how well you have carried out your investigation. Have you conducted your research in a manner that compares to how another researcher would conduct research into the same issues? And more to the point, do your results compare to those of another researcher carrying out the same study? Reliability is also concerned with the research being consistent. You need, in your methodology, to be clear about your procedures and to demonstrate that there has been a consistency throughout your research. Cohen et al. (2000, p117) define reliability as: *a synonym for consistency and replicability over time, over instruments and over groups of respondents. It is concerned with precision and accuracy*. For example, a respondent's age and gender can be measured precisely, whereas measuring the effectiveness of a particular innovation is less precise. When conducting your own research study as part of the MTL, your mentor, coach or tutor will be able to guide you on the most appropriate way for you to ensure reliability for your investigation. This will depend on your methodology, methods and data interpretation.

Insider research

Being a participant in the research process, and having inside knowledge into the area being studied has both advantages and disadvantages. For example, if you are carrying out a research project into an aspect of your classroom practice, you will have a certain amount of knowledge about the classroom and individual characters before you begin your investigation. This could have the effect of inducing a subconscious bias to the study. Compare this example with a researcher coming into your classroom, who has not been to the school before – maybe the researcher is not a teacher, or educational professional. They may well interpret the data in a different manner. It could be argued that they could approach the study in a more objective and detached way, given that they have no experience or knowledge of the area. The question is, of course, will both sets of data be reliable and valid? It is necessary, if you are an insider-researcher, to ask yourself the question: How can I ensure non-biased practice? Using critical friends and your tutor, mentor and coach will help you to remain objective, as will keeping concise and clear notes and reflections as you progress your study. Being critical about your own research style and data collection will help to maintain some objectivity; however, you could also compare your findings to those of similar studies. The advantages of being an insider-researcher are primarily concerned with ease of access to the group being studied. If you are studying your own classroom, you will not need to travel vast distances to access your study area. Another plus point for insider research is that the participants will already know you, so your presence is not likely to be anything significantly different to them. There are some researchers who will argue that this will help to create a research environment that is more natural, as participants are less likely to 'play up to' the researcher.

Triangulation

Triangulation is the term given to the process of comparing several sources of evidence in order to provide an accuracy of the information required. It is linked to validity in that it is a cross-referencing or cross-checking of methods that attempts to compare the methods and that data collected from those methods. For example, if you are carrying out an action research project into an aspect of your classroom practice, you might interview some of the pupils, use your own observations and also hold a focus group. Triangulation occurs when you compare the data from each of the methods and identify where there are commonalities. This is sometimes referred to as multi-method research. It is also possible to triangulate within a single method and some qualitative researchers believe that triangulation may improve the reliability of single-method research (Silverman, 2000, pp98–9)

Summary

This chapter has discussed research and research methodology. It has not given detailed accounts of the issues regarding research, but has offered some general ideas and concepts for discussion. In particular this chapter has addressed areas around:

- different research methods;
- different approaches – e.g. case study, action research and ethnography;
- data management;
- validity and reliability;
- triangulation.

References and **Further reading**

Bassey, M. (2002) Case study research, in Coleman, M. and Briggs, A. (2003) *Research Methods in Educational Leadership and Management*. London: Sage.

Bell, J. (2002) Questionnaires, in Silverman, D. (ed.) (2004) *Qualitative Research: Theory, method and practice*. London: Sage.

Blaxter, L., Hughes, C. and Tight, M. (1996) *How to Research*. Buckingham: Open University Press.

Campbell, A., McNamara, O. and Gilroy, P. (2004) *Practitioner Research and Professional Development in Education*. London: Paul Chapman Publishing.

Cohen, L., Mannon, L. and Morrison, K. (2000) *Research Methods in Education* (5th edn) Abingdon: Routledge.

Coleman, M. and Briggs, A. (2003) *Research Methods in Educational Leadership and Management*. London: Sage.

Cortazzi, M. (2002) Analysing narratives and documents, in Coleman, M. and Briggs, A. *Research Methods in Educational Leadership and Management*. London: Sage.

Elliot, J. (1991) *Action Research for Educational Change*. Buckingham: Open University Press.

Frith, H. (2000) Focussing on sex: using focus groups for sex research. *Sexualities* 3 (3): 275–97.

Hammersley, M. (1990) *Reading Ethnographic Research: A critical guide*. Harlow: Longman.

Hart, E. and Bond, M. (1995) *Action Research for Health and Social Care: A guide to practice*. Buckingham: Open University Press.

May, T. (2001) *Social Research: Issues, methods and process* (3rd edn) Buckingham: Open University Press.

Morgan, D. (1988) *Focus Groups as Qualitative Research*. Beverly Hills, CA: Sage.

Silverman, D. (ed.) (2000) *Doing Qualitative Research: A practical handbook*. London: Sage.

Silverman, D. (2004) *Qualitative Research: Theory, method and practice*. London: Sage.

Strauss, A. and Corbin, J. (1998) *Basics of Qualitative Research: Techniques and procedures for developing grounded theory*. London: Sage.

CHAPTER 6

Developing critical and analytical skills

Chapter Objectives

By the end of this chapter, you will be able to:
- develop a good understanding of critique and analysis skills;
- demonstrate what is meant by reflection and be able to use reflection to enhance your practice and development;
- examine how experiential learning and reflection could complement your own professional development and practice.

Links to standards

This chapter will help you to address the following professional teaching standards.

C3 Maintain an up-to-date knowledge and understanding of the professional duties of teachers and the statutory framework within which they work, and contribute to the development, implementation and evaluation of the policies and practice of your workplace, including those designed to promote equality of opportunity.

C6 Have a commitment to collaboration and co-operative working where appropriate.

C7 Evaluate your performance and be committed to improving your practice through appropriate professional development.

C8 Have a creative and constructively critical approach towards innovation; being prepared to adapt your practice where benefits and improvements are identified.

C10 Have a good up-to-date working knowledge and understanding of a range of teaching, learning and behaviour management strategies and know how to use and adapt them, including how to personalise learning to provide opportunities for all learners to achieve their potential.

C15 Have a secure knowledge and understanding of your subjects/curriculum areas and related pedagogy including: the contribution that your subjects/curriculum areas can make to cross-curricular learning; and recent relevant developments.

P2 Have an extensive knowledge and understanding of how to use and adapt a range of teaching, learning and behaviour management strategies, including how to personalise learning to provide opportunities for all learners to achieve their potential.

Introduction

The MTL requires you to become critical, to use the process of critique both within your own practice and in terms of your professional development. But what is meant by this? What does being critical entail? The following points address the key areas of critical thought.

- Being willing to acknowledge that there are alternatives and to exploring these. Being open-minded.
- Recognising assumptions and being prepared to challenge these where necessary.
- Being sceptical. Approaching conversation and texts with a scepticism and suspicion.
- Distinguishing between opinion and fact: rely on reason rather than emotions.
- Making assertions based on logic and sound evidence.
- Fully controlling one's own thinking. Precise, meticulous and exhaustive thought.

Being willing to acknowledge and explore alternatives

As an MTL student, you will need to fully demonstrate that you are aware that there are other alternatives to your own views and beliefs. It is necessary to be able to be open-minded to as many alternative arguments as possible and to present any conflicting arguments with honesty and as clearly as you would your own. In order to do this, you are likely to need to be able to ask relevant questions and seek clarification where necessary. Being open-minded requires you to evaluate all angles and approaches to a particular problem and if necessary accept new priorities and explanations, even if they are unpopular. For example, you may hold the view that the MTL is a positive step forward to increasing the professional status of teachers, but you need to be aware and appreciate that other teachers will feel differently, and many will feel that the MTL is not necessary, even to the point that CPD is an exploitation of their professionalism. The teachers that hold this view, will probably have the same level of feeling and be able to justify these feelings. Similarly, you may hold the opinion that behaviour is not a contributory factor to learning; however, you need to acknowledge that many teachers are of the opinion that poor learning is a consequence of poor behaviour and they may be able to support their argument with evidence and literature.

Recognising assumptions and challenging where necessary

In order to challenge assumptions, you need initially to be able to recognise the assumptions. Part of this recognition will involve reaching a judgement of the assumption, in particular, in terms of the quality and acceptability of the reasons of the assumption. To do this you will need to consider how the assumption came to fruition in the first place, for example, what led to your head teacher assuming that you wanted to be involved with some school-based research that was being carried out? (Could it be something to do with the fact that at your interview you indicated that you were keen to investigate innovations?) Recognising other people's assumptions is one thing, recognising your own is another, and could be more difficult. For example, you might assume that an elderly relative would be better cared for in a residential care home, where they have access to warmth, food and companionship as opposed to living alone where they will need to ensure they can afford and ensure adequate heating and food and where they need to be able to maintain the property and safety, negotiate stairs, etc. You assume this because it is what you yourself feel would be better for the relative, whereas communal living may be purgatory for them, they may be much happier living in the house in which they have lived all their lives, and which holds their memories. Being critical is all about recognising your assumptions and being able challenge it as necessary.

Being sceptical

Scepticism is being not easily convinced of something or having doubts about something, and is good academic practice, particularly when addressing an area of your professional practice or development. Thinking critically allows you to be sceptical but in a constructive manner. It is neither helpful nor productive to disbelieve everything you hear and see – being sceptical is not about that, it is however about being open and accepting that what you know at a given time might only be part of the real picture. It is easy to regard something as right or wrong, black or white, but of course in reality, the answers are very often at one point along a sliding scale of possibility. It is crucial when being critical and studying at this level, to accept that you may need to pose questions that are quite sophisticated and that address the areas of 'murkiness' around the main issue. Imagine you are talking to two colleagues, one of whom teaches PE, the other teaches maths. If you were to ask the teacher of PE what were the advantages of making athletics compulsory for all pupils, you are likely to obtain quite an in-depth response that may or may not answer your question, but that will offer many other angles to the argument, whereas if you were to ask the teacher of English whether she felt it should be compulsory for all pupils to take part in athletics, you are likely to receive a less involved answer that may offer her views but unsupported by evidence or experience. This example indicates that the more you know about a subject, the more difficult it can be to respond in simple terms to a question about your subject. Being sceptical also requires you to be active as opposed to passive in questioning reason and meaning.

Distinguishing between opinion and fact

Being able to distinguish between fact and fiction is central to developing critical skills. It means not relying on emotions, opinions and feelings, or any of those attitudes that are not based on proof or evidence, but rather to base your findings and reason on fact, that being something which can be corroborated and supported by evidence, either through experience, direct observation or testing. It is something that can be verified and checked for accuracy. Facts that can be checked against reputable sources of evidence are generally considered more believable than personal opinion. However, you must exercise an element of caution, as there are always facts that can later be disproved. It is often difficult to distinguish between fact and opinion when interviewing someone as you can never guarantee that they are telling the truth; similarly, if you send out a questionnaire as part of your research, you can never be 100 per cent sure that the participant is telling the truth. It is sometimes necessary to corroborate your findings with other sources, for example, you may verbally question a selection of people but compare the findings with similar groups. Similarly, you may use newspaper records or other official documents to corroborate with your source. This is very similar to triangulation that was mentioned in the previous chapter. A good skill to begin to develop is knowing what can be proven directly, or being able to identify what is legitimate regarding the supposed fact. On the other hand, it is equally important to be able to recognise opinion. People hold opinions due to their personal evaluations or judgements about something which may or may not be verifiable. Life encounters, experience and knowledge culminate in beliefs and opinions around which many people revolve their lives. It is the point that these opinions are very personal to them that is key to being able to distinguish between opinion and fact. For example, someone may have held the belief that if you go out on a cold and wet day, you are more likely to catch flu. That they have believed this all their life, could result in them believing that it is a fact, when it is really their opinion based on what they were brought up to believe and which they now consider to be true.

Reflective Task

Have a look at the following statements and try to determine which are fact and which are opinion.

*   Most footballers drive expensive cars.
*   If you holiday abroad, you are more or less guaranteed good weather.
*   Fruit and vegetables form an important part of the diet.
*   Great achievers are an inspiration to others.
*   The body needs sleep in order to rest and recuperate fully.
*   The best schools always obtain outstanding Ofsted reports.
*   The worst schools always obtain poor Ofsted reports.
*   Taking risks opens up new opportunities.
*   Taking risks limits the actions that you take.
*   All sportsmen and women are physically fit.

It is much more difficult to ascertain whether these statements are fact or opinion, just by reading them on this page. In reality you are more likely to question the statement-maker to identify the underlying points. When seeking clarification, you are likely to want to know: why, what the main point is, what is meant by it, what would an example be, what difference does it make and how? You can only get this confirmation by questioning.

Making assertions based on logic and sound evidence

Once you have obtained confirmation and clarification, you can assert judgement on the argument. In order to make your assertion you will judge the credibility of the source and using your experience and expertise, you will formulate a logical assumption around the argument. Assertions are normally considered to be statements that are made without justification or evidence (Cottrell, 2005). Being critical requires that any assertions you make are based on logic and robust evidence. Being logical or coming to a logical conclusion means that you deduce your view from a set of reasons.

Making assertions based on sound and robust evidence is equally valid. Evidence can usually be categorised as primary or secondary, primary evidence being the raw data, for example, direct observation and documentary proof of the situation. Secondary evidence refers to the literature written on the primary sources. Being critical requires you to obtain the most relevant source of evidence to support your own arguments. Once you have identified your sources of evidence, you will need to ask several questions of that evidence, such as the following.

* How do we know this is true?
* How reliable is the source?
* Are the examples given truly representative of the whole area?
* Does this match what I already know?
* Does this contradict other evidence?
* What motive might this person have for saying this?
* What are we not being told?
* Are any other explanations possible?
* Do the reasons support the conclusions?
* Is the author's line of reasoning well substantiated by the evidence?

(Cottrell, 2005, p128)

When deciding which evidence to use, ask yourself if it can help to provide a good understanding of the issues and subject. Evidence can either support your argument or offer a contradiction, it may support the subject but not the conclusion, or vice versa. The main thing to bear in mind is that the evidence you source is credible.

Fully controlling your own thinking

Critical thinkers are in full control of their own thinking and thought processes. This requires the development of a set of standards by which one's own thinking is routinely assessed, evaluated and improved as necessary. Being able to critique the work of others also requires you to be able to be self-critical, albeit in a constructive and positive manner. It is good practice to give some thought to how you reach decisions, how you make judgements and how you make the choices that you do, in terms of your practice and development. For example, what influenced your decision to become a teacher? What influences your decisions regarding your work for the MTL? Being in control of your own thinking means that you avoid being intimidated and influenced by the thoughts and actions of others, it also requires you to be able to focus on one or several situations or questions, determining what is important and what is not. Being able to control your own thoughts is something that can be developed over time: if it is something that you have not engaged with, try to spend some time analysing your thought processes and the decisions that you make as a result. The MTL will offer you ample opportunity to do this. Being able to totally control your own thinking relies heavily on a robust self-awareness, you need to be able to recognise and avoid bias; similarly, you will need to develop skills that help you to recognise your own assumptions and prejudices. Only when you can recognise these can you set them aside to acknowledge the points of view of others. Being in control also means that you can resist manipulation and irrational thought. Once developed, critical skills will prevent you from making snap judgements, as you will be able to control your thought patterns to the extent that you will weigh up all the options and have the confidence to suspend judgement and decision if necessary. An old adage is: *Never say yes to anything unless you have fully understood the question and considered the implications.* Thought control allows you to fully appreciate strategies to develop an argument, the formulation of which normally involves identifying and supporting a set of premises or statements. The MTL will, at some point, require you to develop arguments. This is not by any means a negative exercise. It is unfortunate that in our language the word 'argument' is often used to signify bad feelings, poor communication and in certain cases aggressive conversations. Argument in critical thinking terms means identifying your position on a particular subject, offering reasons to support your view, and attempting to persuade others to accept your point of view.

Developing an argument

Some statements and situations are obvious and clearly uncontroversial, for example, someone might say that the weather patterns in the United Kingdom are changing – when they clearly are changing and this is backed up with scientific evidence and observation. More often than not, when you are studying at this level, the arguments that you are faced with are more complex and ambiguous. For example: *pupils benefit from completing homework.* If you are presenting this argument, you need to identify if you agree with this statement. If this is the case, you need to understand why you agree and be able to substantiate this view. If however, you disagree, you need to similarly provide the evidence that supports your view in disagreeing. Let us assume that you feel that homework is beneficial to children. You will need to acknowledge that many people will disagree with you. You will identify who these people are and why they feel in the way that they do. What is their argument? Do you feel that it is valid? Can you see why they feel this way? When you present your argument that homework is beneficial, what is your evidence? What are the implications of this? Which other authors agree with you and what do they say? And so the argument begins to develop. Consider the following statements and consider how arguments could be developed around them.

- The government's influence on education is extremely positive.
- It is vital that all teachers are trained to master's level.
- Head teachers should perform more practical teaching sessions with the pupils.
- Health and safety issues prevent children from having fun and learning about risk.

- Children should, wherever possible, walk to school.
- School meals should be subject to scrutiny from nutritionists.

There will be many views on the subjects that are listed above, and strong and convincing arguments could be attributed to some of the issues. It is important to realise that people who argue against you will have, as far as they are concerned, equally valid reasons for feeling the way that they do, and they will be able to support their views with evidence. This is where critical thinking gets very interesting. It is sometimes necessary to reflect on where the argument might have its foundation, or one of the foundations, for example, the basis for an argument might come from a theory. Equally theories can be arguments by themselves, for example, feminism. In the theory of feminism, the argument is around male domination of women in forms such as physical, political and ideological (Slattery, 2003). There is much literature supporting various arguments around feminism, therefore whichever view you take, you would support it with corresponding literature, but you will need to acknowledge the opposing views and the literature associated with them.

Using critique to support your practice

You need to begin to support your own practice with critical thought. A good way of doing this is being critical in meetings. Normally meetings offer a stage upon which several people can present their own arguments. You can acknowledge the different perspectives given and consider the alternative options. For example, your colleagues will have different responsibilities and therefore will bring different approaches to situations being discussed. This may lead, in some cases, to criticism. Murray and Moore (2006, p47) point out that critical responses are an indication that your work has promoted engagement from others and has stimulated an *active interest*. Criticism can therefore be positive and lead to constructive debate. You will probably hold strong views regarding certain aspects of your teaching role. Do you offer these views in discussions? Or are you more likely to keep them to yourself? Similarly, are you likely to challenge the views of others when they conflict with your own? Being critical about your practice could be interpreted as quite personal and therefore involve and evoke emotions and passion. Studying at this level and in a critical manner, requires you to manage these feelings appropriately, as you need to use logical thought to support your development. This is not to detract from the issue of self-awareness: effective critical thinkers are usually very aware of themselves, of their views and of their motivations and influences. However, what sets them apart is that they can put these aside when and as necessary, and not be influenced by their own beliefs and values.

Practical Task

At the next staff meeting, pay particular attention to the issues raised on the agenda. Give some thought to why particular people are responding in certain ways to the issues raised. If there is an area of tension, try to identify the reasons for this. Talk to staff about their particular view of the meeting agenda and analyse their answers.

Being analytical

'Analysis' is a word often used, but is it understood? Blaxter et al. (1996) suggested that the word 'analysis' can strike fear into people new to research. When we analyse something, we are normally trying to identify an explanation for something and to demonstrate an understanding. The process by which this is done will involve considering various perspectives, concepts and theories. Being analytical is looking at something in a detailed manner, being critical and identifying the strengths and weaknesses. Another way of looking at analysis is to view analytical practice as that which will require you to be able to dissect an issue or situation and critically evaluate its parts, recognising the function and relationship of these parts. There will be some modules within the MTL that specify analysis as part of the assessment. The following examples offer the opportunity to develop a better understanding of the use of analysis when addressing assignment titles.

- *Analyse the impact of peer support within Key Stages 3 and 4.* Firstly, you will need to identify when peer support was introduced and why it was introduced, who introduced it and what were the methods of introduction. Then dissect the issues surrounding the impact and review and critique each. You might choose to compare pupils' results prior to the introduction with results now. You will identify what peer support is and how it is carried out. Is there any significance to the fact that it is carried out at Key Stages 3 and 4? What does the peer support consist of? How has it been received by the children and teaching and support staff? Have any changes to the school improvement plan been made as a result of the introduction of this strategy? You will need to review and critique literature surrounding this issue. For example, has the government offered a perspective? Is there a county council view or agenda for peer support? What research has already taken place in this area, and what were the findings? Once you have addressed these issues in a critical, structured and systematic manner, you will be able to offer an analysis of the impact of peer support.

- *Critically analyse the concept of introducing vocational qualifications to the secondary curriculum.* In this assignment you are being asked to critically analyse a concept. You will therefore need to identify what exactly the concept is and the origin. Why was it introduced? Are there any potential benefits and limitations to the introduction? You will then need to dissect the vocational qualifications aspect and relate your findings to the curriculum. What vocational courses are being delivered? How are they being delivered? Are there any issues surrounding this? For example, are teachers delivering the vocational curriculum, and if so, are they experienced and knowledgeable on the subject? Is the curriculum delivered by other staff, maybe staff that are actually working in the vocational area? What are the positive implications of teaching vocational studies? What are the negative implications? What impact does this have on the local community? The school may well be developing links with local business in order to provide some specialist input. Equally, your analysis may identify the need for the school to begin to form partnerships with local industries and employers. What literature has been written on this subject? What other research has been carried out in the area?

The examples here are intended to give you the opportunity to think around analysis and to identify how, by questioning yourself, you can begin to form a framework for critical analysis. The difference between analysis and critical analysis is subtle but at the same time significant; for example, if you analyse thoroughly you will be critical. However, you are able to provide a descriptive analysis, in which you merely provide a description of something and analyse this. Studying at this level will always require you to provide a critique alongside the analysis.

Using experiential learning

Experiential learning has historically been associated with the adult professional development arena. It is often set in opposition to more formal learning, as its focus is set in the practical situation. The main and distinguishing feature of experiential learning is that it involves the organisation and construction of learning from observations and experiences in the practical area, and furthermore, that these learning opportunities then form the foundations for improved practice within the particular area (Moon, 1999). The opportunity to learn from experience is presented to teachers every day. The important thing is to acknowledge that you are the driver of this learning. The scene is set by the fact that you have a classroom that contains children with whom you will share many experiences. It is up to you to use your classroom as *your* classroom. Learn alongside the children, and learn from the tasks that you jointly perform. Senge (1990) asserted that direct experience provides the most powerful learning platform. The MTL is a work-based master's degree and therefore enables you to use the work you do as part of your teaching role to complement and underpin your professional development. The way in which you capture and transpose this learning is the crux of what is being explored here.

> *The belief that all genuine education comes about through experience does not mean that all experiences are genuinely or equally educative. Experience and education cannot be directly equated to each other.*
>
> (Dewey, 1997, p25)

It therefore seems necessary to identify what is meant by the term 'experience'. In Chapter 4, learning from different scenarios was discussed. It was evident that one could gain a deeper understanding of something from attending a lecture. This could be interpreted by some as an experience. Moon (1999, p22) identifies a *lack of clarity* around the definition of experience, while Kolb (1984) defines experience as something that is physical, involving action and the direct observation of practical skills. Kolb offered a learning cycle that was based around the experiencing of an event from which learning takes place, as presented in Figure 6.1.

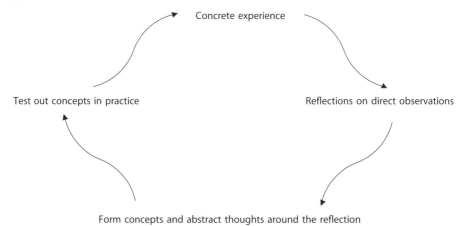

Figure 6.1 Kolb's learning cycle (adapted from Kolb, 1984)

The idea of this learning cycle is that the learner continually transforms from observer to actor, in that they will observe, reflect on the observation and carry out actions based on their learning. For the purpose of this study skills guide and for your learning for the MTL, it is recommended that you establish a framework similar to the one above to enable you to develop your knowledge from experiences encountered in your practice area. It is also recommended that you maintain a learning diary or reflective diary, in which you record your learning experiences. This will help you when you begin to develop your assignments. It is worth bearing in mind that you can learn just as much, if not more, from a bad experience, as you can from a good experience. It might be more difficult to record your feelings following a less than positive situation, but you will reap the benefits at a later date if you are able to record at least the outline of the situation and your reflections. This point is reiterated by Garrick (1999) in his view that what one feels personally about work and the work experience is crucial to any learning that takes place. Which seems to suggest that the way in which you perceive your role could impact on the way in which you learn from your experiences within that role.

Practical Task

During a future lesson in which there are behaviour problems, try to determine why these problems developed. Look at all the options and possibilities when you draw your conclusions regarding this. Be critical in your thought and identify when you reflected in action, and when you reflected on action.

Being reflective

'Reflection' is a word familiar to most of us and which probably conjures up impressions of looking in a mirror or something similar. However, to define reflection in academic terms or in a manner that is related to learning, one may need to apply more thought and attention. When addressing the area of reflection, the work of Donald Schön (1983) provides an informative and inspirational text. Schön advocates two methods of reflection within the practice area: reflection-in-action and reflection-on-action. The difference between these methods appears subtle, yet they need quite different skills in order to effectively achieve true reflection. Schön distinguished between these two processes of reflection by offering the following interpretation.

Reflection-in-action

Also referred to as *knowing-in-action*, Schön referred to reflection-in-action as that process which occurs when activities are carried out without really having to think about them due mainly to the fact that they have been part of daily practice and therefore can be executed spontaneously and with confidence. Reflection-in-action occurs when something surprising or unexpected happens to the normally familiar routine. For example, imagine you are demonstrating to a class how to make a wind chime. You have made hundreds of wind chimes in the past with other classes and you are very confident in carrying out this task. However, on this occasion, your wind chime doesn't work, it gets entangled when hung above the window. You will inevitably question what you did, you will probably check the materials and your technique and mentally compare this occasion with past experiments that have worked. This is essentially reflecting-in-action. You may think quickly that you can try another method to get you out of trouble, as it were. The process that you are going through when you do this is one of critiquing your practical work and is fundamental to reflecting-in-action.

Reflection-on-action

This is a process that is carried out after the event, to identify what you did during the action, and during reflecting-in-action. When you reflect-on-action, you will spend some time once the event has passed, considering what happened and what your actions were. You are likely to reflect on what went well and what went less well. Reflecting back on action will normally offer more time to be able to fully appreciate what led to the situation and what influenced your actions and the actions of others. Robust reflection-on-action could offer the opportunity to improve future actions. For example, imagine that you are a music teacher leading and performing with a student orchestra. While the student orchestra is performing, the players will be reflecting-in-action. Contrastingly, after the performance, they will listen to the recording of their musical pieces and reflect on the performance, probably to identify wrong notes in particular sections of the orchestra, or to find out which section lost time, for example (Schön, 1987).

Case Study

David was a PE teacher in a large secondary school; he had been teaching for three years, over which time he had developed a particular interest in football, rugby and tennis.

He had trained the school football team and coached them to the point where they were entering the National Schools semi-final tournament. David has the support of another PE teacher, Simon, and between them they have been able to motivate and maintain the interest of many good potential young football players from within the school. On the day before the semi-final tournament, David and Simon met with the team to carry out their usual team talk and to assess the fitness level of the players. On the day of the semi-final, the team were feeling confident and began to play really well. David's team scored the first goal and went on to win with a final score of 3–1. During the match both David and Simon were shouting advice from the touchline, encouraging and motivating the players; they were able to see how the match was being played and move players to different positions on the pitch according to what the opposing team were doing. On the following day, David and Simon got the team together and they watched the video of the match, stopping the video at certain places in order to discuss what happened and what would have been a better course of action. The players were able to look back on the match with a different perspective and acknowledge their mistakes, they were also able to observe the positive aspects of the game. David uses this method of reviewing the match as a means of improving the players' awareness for future matches.

Reflective Task

With reference to the case study above, identify where the concepts of Schön are evident. There is opportunity for David, Simon and the team to be critical with the team performance and also to analyse the skills of the players; how might this be done?

The MTL will require you to reflect on your practice throughout the programme. It is recommended that you adopt reflective practice to use during your day-to-day role. You should endeavour to become a reflective practitioner. Maintaining a reflective diary may help you to refine your reflection skills. Forde et al. (2006) point out that reflective practice can underpin your professional development and act as a method of developing professional identity.

By reflecting in and on your practice you can identify areas of limitation or strength. You can address organisational challenges or successes in an open-minded and flexible way. Structured reflection will involve recognising your own views and beliefs and being able to contextualise these, setting them aside if necessary. Reflection also requires you to be honest. Comparing this to the reflection one experiences when looking in a mirror, the image reflected back is a 'warts and all' reflection of the main image. You cannot hide the blemishes. So it is with academic or formal reflection: you should not hide those situations that are less than acceptable as it is often by reflecting on mistakes and errors that you are able to improve future practice.

The work-based nature of the MTL offers you the opportunity to finely hone your reflective skills and in so doing, demonstrate the close relationship between your practice and your continuing professional development. Given that you will be working with a mentor and/or coach within the workplace, it is good practice for you both to begin to recognise and use reflective methods. 'Reflexivity' is a term commonly used at this level of study, and refers to deep reflection, critical or analytical reflection, for example. Some authors (Hatton and Smith, 1995; Kember et al. 1999; Mezirow, 1981) share the view that there are several levels and depths of reflection, reflexivity being generally recognised as the deepest level.

Summary

This chapter has described how important it is to begin to develop academic skills. It has offered the opportunity for you to build on your knowledge in these areas, in particular in terms of supporting your learning on the MTL. The chapter has particularly focused on the areas of:
- critical thinking skills;
- analytical skills;
- reflecting in action;
- reflecting on action;
- experiential learning;
- developing an argument.

References and Further reading

Blaxter, L., Hughes, C. and Tight, M. (1996) *How to Research*. Buckingham: Open University Press.

Cottrell, S. (2005) *Critical Thinking Skills*. Basingstoke: Palgrave Macmillan.

Forde, C., McMahon, M., McPhee, A. and Patrick, F. (2006) *Professional Development, Reflection and Enquiry*. London: Paul Chapman Publishing/Sage.

Garrick, J. (1999) The dominant discourse of learning at work, in Garrick, J. and Boud, D. (eds) *Understanding Learning at Work*. Abingdon: Routledge.

Hatton, N. and Smith, D. (1995) Reflection in teacher education – towards definition and implementation. *Teaching and teacher education,* 11 (1): 33–49.

Kember, D,. Jones, A., Loke, A., McKay, J., Sinclair, J., Harrison, J., Webb, C., Wong, M. and Yeung, E. (1999) Determining the level of reflective thinking from students' written journals using a coding scheme based on Mezirow. *International Journal of Lifelong learning*, 18 (1): 18–30.

Kolb, D. (1984) *Experiential Learning as the Science of Learning and Development*. Englewood Cliffs. N.J.: Prentice Hall.

Mezirow, J. (1981) *Transformative Dimensions of Adult learning*. San Francisco, CA: Jossey-Bass.

Moon, J. (1999) *Reflection in Learning and Professional Development*. Abingdon: RoutledgeFalmer.

Murray, R. and Moore, S. (2006) *The Handbook of Academic Writing: A fresh approach*. Maidenhead: Open University Press/McGraw-Hill.

Schön, D. (1983) *The Reflective Practitioner*. San Francisco, CA: Jossey-Bass.

Schön, D. (1987) *Educating the Reflective Practitioner*. San Francisco, CA: Jossey-Bass.

Senge, P. (1990) *The Fifth Discipline*. London: Random House.

Slattery, M. (2003) *Key Ideas in Sociology*. Cheltenham: Nelson Thornes.

CHAPTER 7

Assessment

Chapter Objectives

By the end of this chapter, you will be able to:
* develop a deeper understanding of different types of assessment;
* identify how to use assessment criteria to structure your assignments;
* demonstrate an increased awareness of the language used in assessment;
* approach your own assessments with more confidence.

Links to standards

This chapter will help you to address the following professional teaching standards.

C2   Hold positive values and attitudes and adopt high standards of behaviour in your professional role.

C3   Maintain an up-to-date knowledge and understanding of the professional duties of teachers and the statutory framework within which they work, and contribute to the development, implementation and evaluation of the policies and practice of your workplace, including those designed to promote equality of opportunity.

C7   Evaluate their performance and be committed to improving your practice through appropriate professional development.

C10 Have a good up-to-date working knowledge and understanding of a range of teaching, learning and behaviour management strategies and know how to use and adapt them, including how to personalise learning to provide opportunities for all learners to achieve their potential.

P2   Have an extensive knowledge and understanding of how to use and adapt a range of teaching, learning and behaviour management strategies, including how to personalise learning to provide opportunities for all learners to achieve their potential.

P5   Have a more developed knowledge and understanding of your subjects' curriculum areas and related pedagogy including how learning progresses within yourself.

P10 Contribute to the professional development of colleagues through coaching and mentoring, demonstrating effective practice, and providing advice and feedback.

E1   Be willing to take a leading role in developing workplace policies and practice and in promoting collective responsibility for their implementation.

E2   Research and evaluate innovative curricular practices and draw on research outcomes and other sources of external evidence to inform your own practice and that of colleagues.

E14 Contribute to the professional development of colleagues using a broad range of techniques and skills appropriate to your needs so that you demonstrate enhanced and effective practice.

Introduction

Assessment has traditionally been based around an examination or essay that addresses the learning outcomes of an assignment. Essays are still used today and demonstrate that the learner is able to commit their work to paper in an appropriate manner. Earlier in this book, you were offered the opportunity to develop the skills necessary for completing an academic essay, which is just one form of assessment. This chapter focuses on other methods and processes of assessment and in so doing, looks at how you can develop the skills necessary to achieve successful assessments.

You need to be able to look upon assessment as part of the learning process – don't be intimidated by or afraid of assessment. The main purpose of assessment is to provide you with a structured opportunity to demonstrate that you can successfully achieve the learning outcomes of a programme or module, thereby reaching the standard required of the award. It is the opportunity for you to be able to articulate your knowledge and learning. Remember the assessment is just as much for your benefit as it is your tutors' and the awarding body. Each module of the MTL will have an assessment attributed to it and therefore it is beneficial to you if you become confident with the process and nature of assessment at the outset. One of the benefits of using your workplace as the main area for your study and having a mentor or coach to support and guide you, is that you can be preparing for the assessment as you are working through the module. Don't leave thinking about, and preparing for, the assessment until the end of the module, but instead get a firm understanding of it right at the beginning; this point cannot be overemphasised. There will be arguments to the contrary, for example, some academic supervisors might feel that it is more beneficial to wait until the latter stages of the module before you begin to plan the assessment. The reason for this is that you could develop a fuller and more abstract understanding of the outline content of the module without worrying about the focus of the assessment learning outcomes. This method does not take into account that some people are scarred from previous failed assessments, whether it was a failed driving test, or a weak assessment in secondary school, and therefore look upon assessment as something which is to be feared. You need to approach the assessments for the MTL in an assertive and confident manner, talk to your coach and tutor about the assessment throughout the module, ask to see other students' work that has been successful, so that you can benchmark the type of standard required, and begin to build a confidence around what it is that you will submit or present at the end of the module. Boud (2001, p56) has defined assessment as having to: *demonstrate that the student has met the requirements of the framework of standards and levels that underpin all programmes.* Assessment is, after all, a mandatory requirement of the awarding body and it is the one process that all students must accomplish successfully.

This chapter will look in detail at portfolios for assessment, it will address what a portfolio needs to look like and what it will need to contain. It will also suggest ways in which you can use your portfolio following assessment as a CPD tool. Presentations will be discussed and you will have the opportunity to identify how you go about planning and carrying out a presentation. Critical discussion is another method of assessment and works in a similar way to a *viva voce*, in that you present your work orally to one or two tutors. This is not an easier option to producing something like an essay or portfolio. You will need to thoroughly understand your topic and be able to vocalise your understanding, being prepared to discuss it critically with your tutors and answering their questions as necessary. Increasingly, universities are being more creative with the way in which assessments are carried out. The modules within the MTL will encompass several methods of assessment. You may even be able to negotiate certain elements of the assessment, which is why it is argued in this book that it is vital for you to understand the criteria for assessment from the beginning of the module.

Approaching assessment – being assessed

The way in which you approach the assessment is fundamental to your success. There are a few dos and don'ts when it comes to your assessment. Have a look at the bullet point lists below and try to address them as you progress through the modules.

Assessment dos
- Start thinking about the assessment from the beginning of the module.
- Be assertive when working out the assessment.
- Remember that the assessment is for your purpose as well as your tutors'.
- Try to understand what the assessment is asking of you at the start of the module.
- Plan for the assessment, organise any research and literature as soon as possible.
- Use your tutor, mentor, coach and critical friend when talking through your assessment.
- If you are able to negotiate your assessment, play to your strength and select a method with which you will be confident.

Assessment don'ts
- Don't panic.
- Don't be intimidated by the assessment; if you have concerns, talk them through with your tutor or coach.
- Don't leave preparing the assessment until the end of the module.
- Don't use the deadline that you have been given. Set your deadline as a week before the official deadline. This will give you time to make any necessary amendments and for your tutor to look over your amended work and give feedback.
- Don't worry what work other MTL students are producing. The MTL is a work-based degree programme, and as you all work in different ways and in different settings, the work produced will be fundamentally different. Similarly, the way in which you interpret the assessment may be different to the interpretations of other colleagues.

You may find it useful to have a look at Table 7.1 which contains some reasons for assessment. This information is taken from PGCE and Cert Ed programmes similar to those undertaken by tutors of the MTL. It is sometimes useful to know what your tutors are being advised.

Table 7.1 Reasons for assessment

Reinforce learning	Test the understanding of the student
Test student skills	Encourage motivation in students
Ensure the maintenance of standards	Offer students an appropriate progression route
Be able to give some indication of the likely future performance of the student	Test the practical performance of the student
Identify how the student applies learning	Provide constructive and helpful feedback to students
Prepare an appropriate learning plan	Qualify

(Adapted from Reece and Walker, 1997)

Types of assessment

There are two types of assessment, formative and summative, and it is beneficial to be able to understand the distinctions between the two types.

Formative assessment

Formative assessment takes place during the module or the programme of study, it is intended to offer the opportunity for students to understand and reflect on their own progress. Formative assessments will take place at certain points during the programme of study and will offer intermittent assessments of the student's work in order that they can address any limitations and build on any strengths prior to submitting work for the summative assessment. Formative assessment could be viewed as more informal in that the feedback given is not likely to be a mark or grade for the work, but rather a discussion or remarks given by the tutor in order that the student can improve. In the case of the MTL, formative assessment is likely to take place on occasions throughout the modules. It will probably involve a discussion with your tutor, mentor or coach and result in some discussed or written feedback on the work you have completed thus far. The feedback will normally be focused on what you will need to do in order to successfully complete the module. This might be a suggestion of changes you make to the work already completed, a set of questions that will aid you in developing a more focused understanding of the outline content of the module, further suggestions for reading, or a discussion of how you can begin to satisfy the learning outcomes. The basic principle of formative assessment is based around the belief that learners need to know what is expected of them before they reach the end of the module. It is a way of providing some continuation of reviewing and checking your work, and give you time to make amendments prior to submitting work for the final assessment and marking.

Summative assessment

Summative assessment is carried out by your tutors and external examiners to ascertain if the work you have finally produced has satisfied the aims, objectives and learning outcomes of the programme. Summative assessment therefore takes place at the end of the particular course of study. There is sometimes a tendency to view summative assessment as something that is bolted on to the end of a programme because that is what happens in education in order to give a mark to the work produced. It is suggested in this book that you use the assessment criteria as something which shape the way in which you plan and carry out your study, and subsequently submit the evidence of your study. The MTL is a modular programme and therefore several formative assessments will be carried out throughout, as you complete each of the modules. The information and guidance exchanged at formative assessment accumulate into a package of knowledge that can be used to support you in submitting your final piece of work for summative assessment. Imagine for one moment, taking part in a master's degree within which there are no structured assessments. How would you know if you had achieved the necessary standard? How would anyone else know if you had achieved the necessary standard? In a wider sense, how could the professional identity and status of teaching be viewed by society in general? Rust (2002) identified that learners expect to be assessed and that many prefer to received a graded mark as opposed to a pass or fail mark. Summative assessment ensures a parity in terms of the quality assurance of a programme; in other words, each participant of the programme will identify with the same assessment criteria.

Learning outcomes

Each module will have a set of learning outcomes which address the criteria necessary to achieve successful completion of the module. The learning outcomes will identify the competencies that the learner needs to be able to successfully demonstrate on completion of the programme. Each chapter within this book begins with a set of intended learning outcomes for the chapter. These outcomes will enable the reader to identify a set of goals or achievements that are possible with the appropriate application to the chapter. Let us consider the learning outcomes for this chapter.

> *By the end of this chapter, you will be able to:*
> * *develop a deeper understanding of different types of assessment;*
> * *identify how to use assessment criteria to structure your assignments;*
> * *demonstrate an increased awareness of the language used in assessment;*
> * *approach your own assessments with more confidence.*

Obviously you are not being assessed on reading the chapters within this book, but having learning outcomes such as this does give you a good idea of how learning outcomes can help you to plan and develop your learning. It is suggested that in reading and further developing the content of this chapter, you will be able to provide the evidence that you can achieve the learning outcomes. The learning outcomes contained within the MTL are likely to ask you to: critically analyse, critically evaluate, reflect analytically, etc. The key is to read the learning outcomes thoroughly and really understand what it is they are asking you to do. For example, if they ask you to critically analyse your school improvement plan, don't merely describe the school improvement plan. Similarly, if the learning outcomes ask you to critically reflect on your practice concerning a particular innovation, then be critical in your reflection: what and why did you do well? What and why did you do less well? How could you improve and what would this involve and influence? It may be appropriate to point out here that, when marking teachers' master's degrees, one of the main themes that is repeatedly fed back to teachers at formative assessment is that they are not being sufficiently critical, when the learning outcomes have clearly stated the need for some form of critique. When tutors are marking your work, the learning outcomes will be used by the markers in order to ascertain if you have successfully met the criteria for the module. You might therefore choose to use the learning outcomes in a similar way, for example, in order to offer a structure for your learning and for the piece of work that you will submit for assessment. If you are writing an essay, you might use the learning outcomes as subheadings for sections of the essay. Alternatively, if you are producing a portfolio you could use the learning outcomes as headings for the different sections of the portfolio. If you use the learning outcomes as a framework and structure, you will offer yourself a really good opportunity to address the overall criteria for the programme. This point is endorsed by Moon (2004, p152) in her view that learning outcomes imply assessment criteria.

Outline content

The outline content of the module is a brief overview or annotation of the key themes of the module. It will offer the student a framework containing some significant points, around which a learning plan can be developed. The outline content is different to the learning outcomes but related, in terms of the outline content offering wider parameters around the subject within which the learning outcomes are featured. The outline content may, for example, indicate that government literature and legislation are addressed, whereas the learning outcomes may indicate that analysis of associated literature is required. The outline content will offer the student wider scope of the module, it will not focus on the assessment but will acknowledge the potential for learning within and around the subject.

Delivery of the modules, as in face-to-face sessions or tutorial sessions, is likely to be planned around the outline content of the module. This gives the tutors a structure for delivery of a tutorial, and it also helps to ensure parity of delivery, which is a requirement of the quality assurance process. The outline content is made available to students at the beginning of the module, thereby offering the student the opportunity to access information or literature for forthcoming delivery sessions. It also enables students to discuss any areas of concern with mentors and coaches prior to working towards the assessment.

Marking criteria: what the marker looks for

Tutors, like students, will approach things differently. The marking criteria and procedures attempt to ensure a level of parity of marking, but tutors will inevitably carry out the process of marking in different ways. For example, some tutors will read through the piece of work submitted for assessment several times prior to reaching a judgement as to how the work has addressed the learning outcomes; other tutors may begin with the learning outcomes and identify as they read the work, whether the students have addressed the criteria. There will be marking criteria to which all tutors will adhere, and these criteria will attempt to address the issue of reliability and validity of marking where several different tutors are involved in marking. The criteria will also assist in the reliability where work is first-marked and second-marked by a different tutor.

The marker needs to be able to identify the piece of work that is being assessed. This may sound obvious, but a surprising amount of portfolios are submitted for marking with no clear identification of whose work it is. A fundamental requirement for the marker is that they are able to identify who has submitted the work for assessment, so make sure that all the work you submit is clearly marked with your name, student number, module title, module number and, if possible, a contact telephone number. Secondly, you will need to adhere to the assessment guidelines for the university. Please pay particular attention to this document as it will help you to present your work in the correct format. The assessment guidelines are likely to indicate how you need to offer your work for summative assessment: if it is an essay, the guidelines will specify the font and line spacing, etc. In the case of a portfolio, the guidelines will demonstrate what qualifies as evidence and how you can present this. The marker will need to be confident that you have addressed the assessment guidelines, and that you have interpreted these appropriately.

Whatever method of assessment is used, the marker will look for evidence that you have met the learning outcomes, and that you are able to organise your learning, as well as the presentation of the evidence of your learning. Your essay will need to be organised; this was addressed in a previous chapter. The portfolio will need to be presented in an organised manner, and this is detailed more fully in the following section. Any critical discussion or reflection will also need to show that you have been able to organise your learning and assessment.

The marker will reach a judgement on your work, which will normally involve ascertaining the level to which you have addressed the learning outcomes, the grammar and punctuation of text, the overall evidence of your learning and the presentation of your work. Once the first marker has performed these tasks, the work will normally be second-marked, where another tutor performs the same process. A selection of work from the whole cohort will then be examined by an external examiner. This process is to verify the first and second markers' work, it is to ensure that the tutors have marked fairly and without bias. It is only after the work has been through this process and presented to the university awards board that the mark can be confirmed.

Portfolios

Presenting a portfolio of work for assessment is a new concept for many teachers, many of whom are more familiar with tests, examinations and essays as a means of having their work marked and assessed. Portfolios are used as assessments within the MTL, therefore it is worth understanding what portfolios are and what an effective portfolio contains. It is probably beneficial at this point to acknowledge the point made by Moon (2004, p160) that the term 'portfolio' relates to a collation of students' work or a learning journal. She goes on to suggest that there is *no one thing called a portfolio and no one way of managing the activity of compiling one.* So before you read any further, remember that your portfolio will look very different to that of your colleagues. Portfolios are very personal: your portfolio will contain information that refers to you and your practice; it will inevitably contain information and knowledge about other people; but it is fundamentally focused on you, therefore it is bound to be different from any other portfolio. If a portfolio is, as Knight and Gallaro (1994) suggest, a collection of students' work presented in a manner that allows for assessment, it seems pertinent to assume that anyone taking part in work-based activities can begin to develop a portfolio. Given that the MTL is firmly based within the workplace, it would seem likely that teachers would use their portfolios for this purpose. The question is however, what constitutes 'work'? As a teacher you will be responsible for planning, implementing and evaluating most of the classroom activities experienced by your pupils. If someone were to ask you to identify how you carried out these activities, how would you be able to provide the evidence of your practice? As an example, giving some thought to your work over the last couple of terms, what projects were you involved in? What work did you carry out as part of this project? Did you carry out any developmental work, for example, did you arrange planning meetings with other staff or parents? Did you work with any external agencies? How did the project develop? What was the outcome? Were there any things that went well? What went less well? Would you do anything differently in the future? If you were to describe your work on this project to another person, maybe to a head teacher or governor, what would you be able to present as evidence of your work? The point being made here is that you are taking part in very complex and high-quality work, and it is often going unrecognised and unrecorded. By developing a portfolio you will be able to collect evidence of projects and other such work as you go along. You can add or remove pieces of evidence from your portfolio as you wish. Evidence can be anything that identifies your practice and your learning. For example, your project may have required you to attend meetings – agendas and minutes from these meetings would count as your evidence. The following list identifies some other types of evidence that you will use to demonstrate your practice.

- *Photographs* – it may be appropriate to photograph such things as new resources, or a display. If you choose to include photographs in your portfolio, and many teachers do, you will need to accompany the photographs with a small account of what they are and why they are pertinent to your learning.
- *Minutes from meetings* – minutes and agendas from meetings can identify your role and responsibilities.
- *Letters* – you may have been required to write to parents or other staff.
- *Pupils' work* – this could demonstrate how your actions have impacted on those you teach.
- *Professional account* – you can write an account of something that you have done.
- *Lesson plans and schemes of work* – plans and schemes can indicate the implementation of what it is you have developed.

- *Action plans* – these can show your planning and development skills and identify time-management qualities.
- *Research report* – you may have carried out a small research project. The report of the methodology and findings can be very good evidence of your learning in the workplace.
- *Handouts and notes from training* – If you carry out any training, INSET, etc., the handouts and notes you make during the training are valuable evidence of your learning.
- *Newspaper and journal articles* – any reports appropriate to your subject or project can count as evidence. However, you will need to identify how the article has impacted on your work. Did it influence what you did? Or did it contradict your work? If you merely photocopy an article and include it in your portfolio without any supporting annotation, the photocopied article only provides evidence that you can use a photocopier.

This list is by no means exhaustive, and your coach, mentor and tutor will be able to advise you as to what is appropriate evidence. One of the most commonly asked questions by teachers when they first begin to develop a portfolio is regarding the appropriateness of evidence. When you begin to develop your portfolio, include everything that you feel might be useful; you can always discuss with your tutor when you next meet, and remove anything that is felt not necessary.

Your portfolio can be used in many other ways and for different purposes. It is a means by which you can reflect on your practice and learn from the work that you have done. Boud (2001) suggested that portfolios are needed in order that students can identify with their formal work-based learning. That the MTL is a work-based programme provides the ideal opportunity for you to use a portfolio to support and focus your learning. It may be useful at this point to consider how the artist demonstrates their learning at the easel. Their paintings are maintained within their portfolio of work, and so it is with the work that you complete. Having a portfolio of your work gives you the opportunity to review and reflect on your practice, it enables you to be critical with your work in a non-threatening manner. It also provides you with a vehicle within which you can transport your evidence from place to place, for instance you may want to transfer information between work and home, and ultimately, to an interview. Imagine attending an interview for a promotion post (having previously identified that the interview panel were happy for you to produce your CPD portfolio) and being able to demonstrate by means of robust evidence, aspects of your practice. It is argued here that you are likely to exude more confidence within the interview knowing that your portfolio that you are about to produce contains a plethora of evidence that supports your claims of knowledge.

For assessment purposes, portfolios offer an excellent opportunity for you to produce a variety of diverse evidence to support the work you do towards the module criteria within the MTL. When using your portfolio in this way, remember that your tutor will mark the portfolio against the learning and marking criteria for the module. Tutors will need to be able to identify that you have produced sufficient and appropriate evidence and supported this with critical reflection of the evidence. When you produce your portfolio to be assessed, ensure that the evidence is secure within the portfolio. If you are using a lever arch file or ring binder, the pages need to be secured within the file. Furthermore, you will need to ensure that your portfolio can be easily identified. Your name, student number and programme details should appear on the first page. Professional accounts and reflective accounts written by you for inclusion with your evidence should be referenced and the reference list and bibliography should be included at the back of the portfolio.

Case Study

David had been an instructor in further education before being successful in applying to complete an initial teacher training course. He had a wealth of experience in land-based occupations and his previous assessments had been predominantly work-based and practical direct observation assessments, mainly through NVQ programmes and practical certificate training courses. One of the first assessments he had to complete for the MTL programme was a portfolio of evidence and reflection. Included in the portfolio was a 2,500-word account of why he felt he would be an effective teacher. The portfolio was to be accompanied by a presentation to the rest of the group. The presentation was a verbal account of the portfolio.

Reflective Task

With regard to the case study, how could David use his previous practical experience and knowledge to support his current study and assessment? What types of evidence could he include in his portfolio? The presentation needed to be a representation of what was in his portfolio; how could he most effectively achieve this?

Presentations

Presentations are used as assessment methods, either in support of a written account or as an assessment method on their own. Presentations are commonly used in teacher training programmes as they offer the opportunity for teachers to demonstrate their skills of talking to a group of people. If you were being assessed by this method, it would be useful to begin to get a firm understanding of the subject of your presentation at the outset. Be confident about what it is you are presenting as you may be questioned on some of the content. If you are confident about the topic, you are more likely to be able to verbally articulate this in a strong and convincing way. From the start of the module, be clear on how the presentation will develop. For example, will you prepare a PowerPoint presentation or use some other form of information technology? If so, make sure that the necessary equipment will be provided for you. Also, you will need to back up your data for the presentation. There is nothing worse than planning and preparing for a presentation, saving it to memory stick or on the hard drive, then the night before the presentation, when you are going through your talk, being unable to locate the data or locating the data, and being unable to display it on the screen.

Presentations are prepared in much the same way as an essay or portfolio. The information is gathered from whichever source, either as a research project or from literature, and then arranged in a manner that can be presented to a number of people. While gathering the information, it is advisable to have some sort of system within which references can be stored. Certain information may be used within the presentation as a handout or as a slide on the screen. The collection of evidence and supporting literature is the first stage. This is followed by the organisation stage. Putting the information into some sort of order, at this point you would need to begin to talk about your project, get used to discussing this with colleagues and friends, ask them to question you about your speech, and when they do, use what they say constructively. Time your presentation talk; you will probably have a set time allocation for the whole of your presentation and this will either include or exclude the time for questions. Be clear about this, as the presentation planning will need to take into account any questions. When planning the section in the presentation for questions you will need to identify if you want to lead the questions, in which case you will need to plan some question prompts. If your presentation offers an open questions section, then you will need to be prepared for anything. If handouts are to be given to the audience, decide when you want to give them out. If you give them out at the beginning, the audience can use them to write notes on, which may help in their understanding of what you are saying. However, this does offer the opportunity for them to be distracted from the talk itself. Alternatively, you could give the handout at the end of the presentation; when this is the case, you are really giving them as a reinforcing tool rather than a document which supports learning. The audience are less likely to connect with any handouts that are given at the end of the presentation, unless it is specified that they need to address them in some way.

For the presentation, you should have prepared well, and practised in front of other people, so that you are confident with what you are saying. Remember, that it is likely that, apart from any tutors, mentors and coaches, you are likely to be the most knowledgeable person about the subject in the room. Before you begin to speak, try to give eye contact to as many people as possible. Take your time – what seems to be a long time to you is not really very long at all to the audience – and similarly, when you speak, if it seems that you are speaking too slowly, you have probably got the speed for your presentation about right for the audience. Although you will probably have some prompt cards or notes for yourself, refer to them only when necessary, don't read from them. If you use the PowerPoint slides to give you your prompt, don't read word for word from the PowerPoint slide. Project your voice to the back of the group, and give intermittent eye contact throughout to all the members of the group or audience. If you reach a point in the presentation where you simply dry up or lose concentration, or if you suddenly become speechless with nerves – it happens to most people at some time – ask members of the group for examples or ideas on what it is that you are discussing. This will give you some time to regroup your thoughts and composure. You could suggest that the group discuss in pairs a certain aspect of your theme. Nobody in the group will object if you need to take few seconds break for a drink of water; again, it might seem a long time to you, but it really is not a big deal for the audience. The people to whom you are talking will need to know when you want them to join in, when it is acceptable for them to ask questions, so tell them at the beginning. Do you want them to interact from the start? Or would you prefer it if they joined in at the end?

The presentation is an assessment of the way in which you can verbalise your knowledge to a group of people and answer questions verbally. The tutors who are marking your presentation are likely to be concerned with what you have to say, rather than the way in which you say it. However, you will need to be understood by the audience and you will need to demonstrate a clear presentation style.

Practical Task

Prepare a short presentation for a small group of your colleagues or friends about your studies. Try to anticipate the questions that they are likely to ask you. Prepare your presentation in PowerPoint and save it to a file on your PC desktop. Carry out this presentation and ask your colleagues for constructive feedback.

Summary

This chapter has offered the opportunity to address the area of assessment. It has done this by discussing some of the different methods of assessment, both formative and summative. In particular, this chapter has:
- offered suggestions of how to use assessment criteria as a framework for planning the assignment;
- addressed ways to improve confidence when being assessed;
- discussed the issues surrounding portfolios and presentations.

References and **Further reading**

Boud, D. (2001) Creating a work-based curriculum, in Boud, D. and Solomon, N. (2001) *Work-Based Learning: A new higher education?* Buckingham: Open University Press.

Knight, M. and Gallaro, D. (1994) *Portfolio Assessment: Applications of portfolio analysis.* London: University Press of America.

Moon, J. (2004) *A Handbook of Reflective and Experiential Learning: Theory and Practice.* Abingdon: RoutledgeFalmer.

Reece, I. and Walker, S. (1997) *Teaching Training and Learning: A practical guide.* Tyne and Wear: Business Education Publishers.

Rust, C. (2002) The impact of assessment on student learning: How can research literature practically help to inform the development of departmental assessment strategies? *Active Learning in Higher Education.* 3 (2): 128–44.

CHAPTER 8

The practicalities of studying in the twenty-first century

Chapter Objectives

By the end of this chapter, you will be able to:
- identify issues relating to the future of CPD for teachers;
- develop a deeper understanding of current research on teachers' CPD;
- demonstrate an understanding of lifelong learning and work-based learning;
- be able to understand more fully the concept of integrated and collaborative practice.

Links to standards
This chapter will help you to address the following professional teaching standards:.

C3 Maintain an up-to date knowledge and understanding of the professional duties of teachers and the statutory framework within which you work, and contribute to the development, implementation and evaluation of the policies and practice of your workplace, including those designed to promote equality of opportunity.

C7 Evaluate your performance and be committed to improving your practice through appropriate professional development.

C8 Have a creative and constructively critical approach towards innovation: being prepared to adapt your practice where benefits and improvements are identified.

C10 Have a good, up-to-date working knowledge and understanding of a range of teaching, learning and behaviour management strategies and know how to use and adapt them, including how to personalise learning to provide opportunities for all learners to achieve their potential.

C35 Review the effectiveness of your teaching and its impact on learners' progress, attainment and well-being, refining your approach where necessary.

C37 Establish a purposeful and safe learning environment which complies with current legal requirements, national policies and guidance on the safeguarding and well-being of children and young people so that learners feel secure and sufficiently confident to make an active contribution to learning and to the school. Identify and use opportunities to personalise and extend learning through out-of-school contexts where possible making links between in-school learning and learning in out-of-school contexts.

P2 Have an extensive knowledge and understanding of how to use and adapt a range of teaching, learning and behaviour management strategies, including how to personalise learning to provide opportunities for all learners to achieve their potential.

> **P5** Have a more developed knowledge and understanding of your subjects, curriculum areas and related pedagogy including how learning progresses within yourself.
>
> **P10** Contribute to the professional development of colleagues through coaching and mentoring, demonstrating effective practice, and providing advice and feedback.
>
> **E1** Be willing to take a leading role in developing workplace policies and practice and in promoting collective responsibility for their implementation.
>
> **E2** Research and evaluate innovative curricular practices and draw on research outcomes and other sources of external evidence to inform your own practice and that of colleagues.
>
> **E14** Contribute to the professional development of colleagues using a broad range of techniques and skills appropriate to your needs so that you demonstrate enhanced and effective practice.

Introduction

This chapter will discuss the implications for the future of teachers' CPD. It will offer the opportunity for you to reflect on current development and practice, and in so doing, enable you to give some thought on the future of qualifications for the children's workforce, both inside and outside the school environment. The TDA (2008, p4) has been clear in its view that in order to be effective, CPD *should be directly relevant to the participants, clearly identify intended outcomes, take account of previous knowledge and expertise, model effective teaching and learning strategies, and include impact evaluation.*

The agency further suggests that each individual school will approach CPD in a different way.

There are significant areas and discourse that impact on teachers' CPD and influence them in their decisions to engage with, or disengage from, CPD. Government policy is a key influence as it underpins the national legislative framework. However, it would appear that several tensions exist between government policy and the way in which teachers view and perceive CPD. That teaching is transforming into a master's-level profession provides implications for the way in which existing teachers approach and engage with CPD. For example, newly qualified teachers will be exiting from initial teacher training with the MTL, and apart from a few teachers who have obtained an MA or MSc, the vast majority of teachers will hold a BA or BSc. This has the potential for creating ambiguity and animosity within schools. One way of trying to prevent this is to offer the current and existing teachers who are currently qualified to BA or BSc level, the opportunity take part in CPD that is accredited at master's Level. This will have implications for universities, local authorities and schools, in that the training and development opportunities will need to be developed, delivered and assessed at an appropriate level.

The Government Green Paper: *Learning and Teaching: A strategy for professional development* (DfEE, 2001), in which the government set out its plans and priorities in respect of the professional development of teachers and the proposed impact on school improvement, identifies the way in which teacher development is viewed at government level. At the time the document was prepared, it was felt that access to CPD for teachers depended to a significant degree on the culture of the particular school in which they were working. The government have further identified that schools will become effective *learning communities, where the vision and commitment of the head teacher, supported by the senior management team and placing the professional development of their staff, is at the heart of their approach to school improvement* (DfEE, 2001).

A more recent government publication is *Higher Standards, Better Schools for All: More choice for parents and pupils* (DfES, 2005), in which the government sets out its strategy in respect of:

* tailoring education to the needs of the individual child;
* placing parents at the centre of the decision-making process regarding their child's learning;
* empowering individual teachers and schools.

Education in the twenty-first century in the United Kingdom is driven largely by policy and focused on outcomes which could, albeit in part, have resulted in teachers' identities being in flux (Stronach et al., 2002). In respect of identities, Wenger (1998) argued that identities are constructed by people engaging actively within their particular community of practice. These communities are multi-functional, and are constructed by people learning, collaborating and negotiating, functions which significantly influence the formation of identities. It could be interpreted therefore that teachers' professional identity is formed, albeit in part, by the fact that they belong to a group or community otherwise known as 'teachers'. Britzman (1992, p23) agrees with this by suggesting that identity is a *constant social negotiation that can never be permanently settled or fixed*. Similarly, Hargreaves (1994) found that the 'new professionalism' of teaching is underpinned by a shift from the traditional practices of teacher authority and autonomy, towards a culture of working collaboratively with colleagues and negotiation of roles and responsibilities. These views would appear to be in conflict with the performance management model which underlines the teachers' autonomy for such areas as professional development. Mahony and Hextall (2000) suggested that there is much debate and deliberation, and not an insignificant amount of literature on the reconstruction of both the teaching profession and teachers as individuals. They further suggest that:

> the literature echoed the divergence between, empowered, up-skilled flexible images of teaching on the one hand and occupational intensification, fragmentation and differentiation on the other. Teachers may experience both the positive and negative aspects of these features at the same time.
>
> (Mahony and Hextall, 2000, p102)

More recently, Forde et al. (2006, p12) in examining the key issues in the definition of teacher's identities, found that, over the years, discourses of teacher identity have changed, from the *individual identity of the early 20th century to the managerially imposed identity of the 21st century.* They further argue that teachers need to reclaim some of the previous agendas in order that teachers can be at the centre of decision-making processes and the teaching profession and the professional community can be, once again, at the centre of educational policy. This is in conflict with the point made by Whitty (1997) in that the self-management of schools has led to the increased involvement of teaching staff in the decision-making process. Historically, when schools were managed by central government, there was a connectedness between senior school managers and other staff. Issues were dealt with under the auspices of 'fighting a common cause'. Now, however, with self-governing schools, a schism has developed which has resulted in staff no longer considering the head teacher as a partner in the decision-making process.

Senge (1990) further suggested that some businesses and companies resist encouraging their staff to develop as it is difficult to measure how the professional development of the individual contributes to the overall effectiveness of the company. He also felt that some managers might feel threatened by the development of individual members of staff, a point which concurs with the issues raised earlier in terms of newly qualified teachers having the MTL working with existing teachers and managers who may not be qualified at this level.

> *One of the greatest resources a school has is its staff, so the education of teachers themselves and the way their work is defined are therefore of the utmost importance.*
> (Mahony and Hextall, 2000, p1)

Campbell et al. (2004, p13) argued that teachers' CPD is now a *high profile, politically hot issue,* while Kydd (1997) considered it crucial, both from the point of view of the individual teacher, and in terms of the overall effectiveness of the organisation. CPD would certainly appear to have a higher place on the political agenda in particular in terms of current school improvement plans, and performance management models.

This chapter will identify some key areas associated with teachers' CPD and in doing so will offer teachers new to the MTL qualification the opportunity to reflect on the most effective methods of CPD for themselves.

Lifelong learning

A culture of lifelong learning can be developed within the workplace by effective management of staff CPD (Blandford, 2000). For teachers in today's schools and in the schools of the future, CPD and lifelong learning will become an integral part of their role. There is some evidence in terms of the numbers of teachers engaging with Master of Arts degrees and Master of Science degrees, that CPD is beginning to form part of the daily routine of some teachers, but if schools are to become learning communities where the training and development needs of all staff are catered for, many more of the existing teachers need to address their CPD and in doing so, give themselves the opportunity to develop their knowledge and understanding, skills and ability. The government paper that focuses on lifelong learning, NAGCELL (1997), identifies that a barrier to arguably one of the main methods of lifelong learning – research – is the language of research itself. Research has been discussed in Chapter 5. The paper highlights the government's support for lifelong learning. As schools become communities of learning for staff, it is likely that teachers will be carrying out CPD activities with teaching assistants and other members of the school workforce. Where this is happening, many schools have sought accreditation for the CPD activity from a university. The accreditation will be at a level appropriate to each member of the whole school workforce, for example, teachers' CPD will be accredited at level 7 or master's level, while teaching assistants and other undergraduate staff will be taking part in CPD that is accredited at level 4, thereby enabling access to foundation degrees.

Lifelong learning is a process that is aided by the use of reflective or learning diaries. These diaries offer the opportunity for teachers to maintain notes of situations and occasions that occur spontaneously and that they can later reflect on. Diaries can be kept for long periods of time and provide an opportunity for teachers to archive and keep details of their skills and knowledge, which could be used in the future and when sharing practice with colleagues or managers. Certificates and details of training courses can be kept alongside evidence from practice, which offers an opportunity for comparison and critical reflection as well as self-analysis. Schools that invest in the lifelong learning of staff are more likely to benefit from staff being up to date with current government initiatives and new working practices. Similarly, the individual teacher is likely to develop more confidence as they build on their knowledge and skills base. The old adages *You never stop learning,* and *You're never too old to learn,* seem to reflect the impetus of lifelong learning, the key to which is looking upon initial training and initial qualification as the start of the learning rather that the end.

Work-based learning

Learning at work was something of an oxymoron to many businesses, managers and employers as they struggled to move away from the old concept that learning was some-thing people did at schools, colleges and universities, and work was something people did for a wage at their place of employment. The idea of combining the two activities seemed to some to be too much of a conflict. Even today, some employers and managers find it difficult to understand that the two areas can be successfully combined. Equally, some universities have, in the past, focused their research and scholarly activities within the university and academic institutions. Universities today are more confident in forming partnerships with employers and business in order to support learning in the workplace. The case for work-based learning attempts to quash the concept of learning and working as being separate entities. Boud and Garrick (1999, p5) stated that:

> In this climate, learning has become too important to be left to educational institutions and in-house training departments . . . it is too intimately connected with productivity and the operation of contemporary enterprises. Understanding of workplace learning is required at all levels and in more diverse ways that ever before . . . It is about investment

> *in the general capabilities of employees as well as the specific and technical. And it is*
> *about the utilisation of their knowledge and capabilities wherever they may be needed.*

It seems from this quotation that learning in the workplace is best served by a combined approach. If learning is too important to leave to educational institutions, it seems pertinent to suggest that training institutions and employers need to work together in order to develop and deliver work-based learning. This point is further supported by Boud et al. (2001, p4) who found that *partnerships are required to enable infrastructure to support learning.* Globalisation, funding, competition and changes to work practices and educational processes have provided challenges for partners who work together in providing work-based learning. Financial and economic issues impact on this method of learning, as each of the partners is likely to be funded by a different body. Take, for example, accredited work-based learning within a school, the staff working for the university providing the accreditation and support will be funded by their employer, and will draw down funding for the students from either the Training and Development Agency (TDA) or the Higher Education Funding Council for England (HEFCE), whereas the school staff will be employed by the school and any funding will be sought from the local authority. This provides the opportunity for competing funding issues and for conflicts of interests in terms of paying for the training.

Quality assurance implications are sometimes cited as a reason for work-based learning to be lacking in the robustness of classroom-led training. In the case of accredited work-based learning, the programmes engaged in will normally have been through a process of accreditation and validation, thereby offering a level of quality assurance; however, the challenge is for those courses that do not have accreditation attached to them. Boud and Solomon (2001, p218) further suggest that the *credibility of work based learning programmes is not solely a function of the contribution of the university. Partner organisations have a crucial and necessary role to play, complementary to the educational institution.* So again, this points to successful work-based learning depending on successful partnership working and collaboration. The future of learning in the workplace therefore relies on the organisations involved working effectively together for the benefit of both the learners and the workplace. Back in 1989 Gerald Dearden directed a project called *learning while earning* which was the first occasion that accredited work-based learning had been approached by universities. Thankfully, today, many universities have invested considerably in work-based learning and several have dedicated departments and faculties to learning in the workplace, an indication probably, of the direction of future adult learning.

Integrated practice

Historically, agencies working with children and with the children's workforce have carried out their practice in isolation and without any cross-referral between agencies. For example, teachers might never have communicated with social workers, and vice versa, where the child they were supervising, albeit at different times, was the same individual. The Children Act 2004 set out a request for every local authority to develop a post that was responsible for the co-ordination of children's services. The government called for interconnectedness and joined-up thinking with regards to those caring for, and with responsibility for, children. The concept of agencies sharing information and working together seems obvious; however, it was the Laming Report of 2003 following the death of Victoria Climbié and, more recently, the death and subsequent investigations into the death of Baby P, that have secured the future of cross-professional working, collaborative practice, and formalised the government's agenda for child protection. The beginning of the twenty-first century saw the development of multi-agency practice, this is evident in such initiatives as Sure Start, the anti-poverty children's project that was the first real attempt to conjoin such services as health visitors, teachers, social workers, psychologists, therapists and counsellors. This initiative may well act as the model for other children's services at the point of contact with the child.

This book is concerned with integrated practice, in terms of the education and training of those within the children's workforce. Enabling multi-professional teams to work together with the common goal of protecting and nurturing children would seem to offer the optimum working practice. However, the way in which multi-professional teams are constructed, managed and co-ordinated offers challenges for training providers and employ-ers. There is the potential for tensions in terms of pay and conditions as the many professionals working together could well be working to very different employment contracts and have different salaries. This could cause resentment if the salaries differ to a significant degree. The way in which language is used could differ between teams. It will be very important for inter-professional teams to be aware of this in terms of using the professional jargon and abbreviations that teams so often use. Managers of cross-profes-sional teams will need to be aware of the challenges in communication and seek to identify ways to overcome misinterpretation and misunderstanding. There could also be tensions in terms of qualification and status. The qualifications frameworks for the different professionals working together would probably be quite different. As an example, police officers' initial training in some areas is done at Foundation degree level, whereas, initial teacher training is becoming a master's-level profession. This is quite a significant difference in terms of the level of initial training that potentially the members of the same team could have experi-enced. Associated to this, but not exclusively related, is the issue of status. A particular professional may have a certain status within the discipline that they practice, which could be as a result of qualification or time of service. However, when they then become a member of a multi-professional team, this status may not be recognised.

University campuses have traditionally been the domain of separate faculties. Many of these faculties have been centred on a particular profession, i.e. the faculty of education, faculty of health, faculty of business, etc. If universities are to embrace true multi-professional practice, strategies should be introduced to enable cross-faculty practice and collaboration. This will have implications for the way in which staff work together on projects concerning the children's workforce, as often different and competing cultures may exist within these faculties. Anning et al. (2006) reported on the MATCh project, which was a two-year research project carried out at the University of Leeds. The aim of the project was to *explore the daily realities of delivering public and voluntary sector services by multi-agency teamwork* (Anning et al., 2006, p10). This research recognised the contributions to theory of Wenger and Engestrom. Wenger's communities-of-practice model has been discussed earlier in this book. Engestrom had at the heart of his theory the premise that whenever tasks are redesigned or realigned, conflict is likely to occur. He felt that these conflicts must be debated openly, thereby enabling new forms of knowledge and practice (Engestrom, 1999). The MATCh project identified that the individuals being studied felt that it was very important when working in a multi-disciplinary team, to develop an understanding of each other within the team. It was also felt that a shared humour helped to cement team relationships. The project also identified that some team workers felt that there was the potential for a 'watering down' of expertise and skills across the team as generalised practices became more prevalent.

Multi-professional and cross-collaborative working will be developed further over the coming years; quite what shape it will take will depend on the different professionals and their ability to work in a conjoined manner but what does seem certain is that employers and training providers need to develop plans for this model of working.

Practical Task

Log on to the website: **www.dscf.gov.uk** and find out what the government agenda is for lifelong learning and work-based learning. Have a look at the Common Assessment Framework on **www.dscf.gov/ISA/sharing_assessment/caf.cfm** and give some consideration to how this assesses children's needs. On a blank piece of paper, write down all the professionals that could potentially be involved in the care of a child. What would be the implication for the training and CPD of these people?

Policy

The introduction by the government of the performance-management model has several implications for teachers' CPD. In particular, it has identified that teachers will receive an annual appraisal which will address issues surrounding teachers' CPD needs and assessment of their performance. The TDA (2008) has identified that each school will develop its own CPD policy, taking into account the individual needs of the school. There is the potential for tension and conflict here. For example, if a teacher wishes to take part in a certain CPD programme, say an accredited university-led course, that is not part of the school CPD policy, would that teacher be supported in their CPD by the head teacher? It would seem pertinent to suggest that the head teacher will need to develop the school CPD policy in response to certain needs within the school and not as a response to individual teachers. The TDA has offered an example of what a CPD policy might include, the main features of which are as follows.

The CPD policy is:

* evidence based;
* based on the collective vision of improving practice;

- acknowledging of the previous knowledge, experience and qualifications of staff;
- focused on enabling the whole school workforce to develop their skills, knowledge and understanding;
- part of a long-term and sustainable plan that offers staff the opportunity to apply what they learn to practice, and in doing so, evaluate and reflect on their learning;
- designed to prompt enquiry, questioning and problem-solving;
- intended to benefit individual members of staff and the school as a whole.

(TDA, 2008)

It seems likely therefore that future CPD will be school-based and driven by the needs of the school, and one could assume where possible, be beneficial to individual staff. The head teacher's role in managing and developing CPD is crucial to the success of the development of staff. It would also seem likely to suggest that schools could become the centre or learning community for practitioners from other professions to join with school staff in participating in multi-professional CPD.

Assessment

In the previous chapter, the use of portfolios was discussed as a means of collating and presenting evidence and reflection. In the future, portfolios are likely to be electronic. There are currently software packages available that allow practitioners to complete CPD portfolios relatively easily. An electronic portfolio is relatively simple to set up within a file on your own PC, by saving to your CPD e-file the evidence that would have been submitted in paper format. The advantage of an e-portfolio would be that data could be saved easily and securely, information could be sent to tutors or mentors with relative ease and the e-portfolio could save more data and information than could reasonably be stored in a paper file.

The assessment process is likely to be more flexible in future as work-based learning comes to the fore. The challenge for universities is to ensure that the appropriate level is accomplished by students using the model of work-based learning. Assessing students' critical and analytical knowledge and understanding by asking them to submit an essay is, in a way, quite straightforward. Assessing the same qualities by other modes of assessment is quite a challenge, particularly if university staff are not familiar with assessing work-based practice, particularly at level 6 and above.

Research

Educational action research will become more common as teachers are encouraged to investigate their practice in a structured and systematic fashion. Teachers will be researchers and many will need support and guidance initially to develop an appropriate methodology. Sharing best practice is something which is not new in schools, but the people who share that practice will be. Earlier in this chapter, integrated and collaborative practice was discussed and the holistic needs of the individual child were central to the provision of support for that child. In terms of research, teachers could well be carrying out research projects with social workers, police officers, parents, health visitors and other professionals concerned with the safety and care of the child. The key to the future of educational research is to breach old boundaries with an assertive confidence. One particular pitfall that teachers could face when it comes to carrying out action research is to assume that all research should be carried out by teachers and in the school. Other professionals in other locations should be included, enabling collaboration, which will add considerable value to any investigation that is being carried out. This is not to detract from the fact that classroom-based research will and must continue as schools become more focused communities of learning, but the point here is that this is not exclusively the case.

Case Study

Jake is a 13-year-old boy who has lived at home with his mother, father and a younger and an older brother. Throughout his schooling, Jake was always pleasant and a very popular member of each teaching group that he entered. Jake's family were always supportive of him and the school, so when his mother died suddenly, both teachers and pupils at the school were equally devastated. As time went on, Jake began to struggle at school, he began to play truant and when he reached Year 7, he had a significant disciplinary record and little hope of achieving decent exam grades. The teachers who had known Jake from the beginning of his secondary education were disappointed and upset, as they had witnessed the change in him as an apparent result of his mother's death. Jake left school without gaining any employment or admission to further education.

Reflective Task

Using the case study above, imagine that you are Jake's head of year prior to his leaving school. You knew him before his mother died and you had a very good and successful learning relationship with him. How did you feel then, when you learnt that social workers were working with Jake and his younger brother just after his mother's death, as he had been causing problems within the neighbourhood in which he lived? How did you also feel when you found out that Jake had been seeing a child psychologist to try to help him to come to terms with his mother's death? What were your feelings when his father informed you that the entire family had received counselling owing to the fact that his wife had had a traumatic death? And how did you feel when you found out that the police youth inclusion officer was also monitoring Jake as he had begun to steal from local shops and business premises?

Summary

This chapter has used recent research and policy together with informed knowledge and experience in offering some ideas and notions of how teachers will develop in the future. The focus of this book has been the MTL and how teachers can adapt their skills in order to successfully complete the master's degree. However, consideration needs to be given to how this influences the practice area and current teachers, who may not have access to the MTL, but who may be able to carry out master's-level CPD. In particular, this chapter has identified briefly the issues surrounding the areas of:

- lifelong learning;
- work-based learning;
- integrated practice;
- policy and research.

In order for teachers to develop a more in-depth understanding of the influences on the future of teachers' development, the literature identified in the reading list at the end of this chapter should be addressed.

References and Further reading

Anning, A., Cottrell, D., Frost, N., Green, J. and Robinson. M. (2006) *Developing Multiprofessional Teamwork for Integrated Children's Services*. Maidenhead: Open University Press/McGraw Hill.

Blandford, S. (2000) *Managing Professional Development in Schools*. Abingdon: Routledge.

Boud, D. and Garrick, J. (1999) *Understanding Learning at Work*. Abingdon: Routledge.

Boud, D. and Solomon, N. (2001) *Workbased Learning: A new higher education*. Buckingham: Open University Press.

Boud, D., Solomon, N. and Symes, C. (2001) New practices for new times, in Boud, D. and Solomon, N. (2001) *Workbased Learning: A new higher education*. Buckingham: Open University Press.

Britzman, D.P. (1992) The terrible problem of knowing thyself: Towards a post structural account of teacher identity, in Goodson, I. and Hargreaves, A. (1996) *Teachers' Professional Lives*. Abingdon: RoutledgeFalmer.

Brown, P. and Lauder, H. (1997) Education, globalization and economic development, in Halsey, A., Lauder, H., Brown, P. and Wells, A. (eds) *Education: Culture Economy Society*. Oxford: Oxford University Press.

Campbell, A., McNamara, O. and Gilroy, P. (2004) *Practitioner Research and Professional Development in Education*. London: Paul Chapman Publishing.

Couldron, J. and Smith, R. (1999) Active location in teachers' construction of their professional identities. *Journal of Curriculum Studies*, 31 (6): 711–26.

Danaher, G., Schirato,T. and Webb, J. (2000) *Understanding Foucault*. London: Sage.

Day, C. (1999) *Developing Teachers: The challenges of lifelong learning*. Abingdon: FalmerPress.

Day, C. and Bakioglu, A. (1996) Development and disenchantment in the professional lives of head teachers, in Goodson, I and Hargreaves, A. (eds) *Teachers' Professional Lives*. Abingdon: Routledge-Falmer.

Dearden, G. (1989) *Learning While Earning: Learning contracts for employees*. London: Learning From Experience Trust.

DfEE (1997) *Excellence in Schools*. White Paper. London: HMSO.

DfEE (1998) *Teachers Meeting the Challenge of Change*. Green Paper. London: HMSO.

DfEE (2001) *Learning and Teaching: A strategy for professional development*. Green Paper. London: DfEE.

DfES (2005) *Higher Standards, Better Schools for All*. White Paper. London: DfES.

Elliott, J. (1991) *Action Research for Educational Change*. Buckingham: Open University Press.

Engestrom, Y. (ed) (1999) *Perspectives on Activity Theory*. New York: Cambridge University Press.

Forde, C., McMahon, M., McPhee, A. and Patrick, F. (2006) *Professional Development, Reflection and Enquiry*. London: Paul Chapman Publishing.

Fullan, M. and Hargreaves, A. (1992) *Teacher Development and Educational Change*. Abingdon: Falmer Press.

Gardner, P. (1995) Teacher training and changing professional identity in early 20th century England. *Journal of Education for Teaching,* 21 (2): 191–217.

Goodson, I. (2001) *Professional Knowledge: Educational studies and the teacher*. Buckingham: Open University Press.

Hargreaves, A. (1994) *Changing Teachers, Changing Times*. New York: Teachers College Press.

Kydd, L. (1997) Teacher professionalism and managerialism, in Kydd, L., Crawford, M. and Riches, C. (eds) *Professional Development for Educational Management*. Buckingham: Open University Press.

Lawn, M. and Grace, G. (1987) *Teachers: The culture and politics of work*. Abingdon: Falmer Press.

Mahony, P. and Hextall, I. (2000) *Reconstructing Teaching: Standards, performance and accountability*. Abingdon: RoutledgeFalmer.

McKenzie, J. (2001) *Changing Education*. London: Prentice Hall.

NAGCELL (1997) *Life long learning*. London: HMSO.

Oldroyd, D. and Hall, V. (1997) Identifying needs and priorities in professional development, in Kydd, L., Crawford, M. and Riches, C. (eds) *Professional Development for Educational Management*. Buckingham: Open University Press.

Ozga, J. and Lawn, M. (1981) *Teachers Professionalism and Class*. Abingdon: Falmer Press.

Plummer, K. (2001) *Documents of Life 2*. London: Sage.

Power, M. (1997) *The Audit Society*. Oxford: Oxford University Press.

Pricewaterhouse Cooper (2001) *Teacher Workload Survey*. Final Report. London: DfES.

Senge, P. (1990) *The Fifth Discipline*. London: Random House.

Sinclair, J., Ironside, M. and Seifert, R. (1993) Classroom struggle? Market oriented education reforms and their impact on teachers' professional autonomy, labour intensification and resistance. Paper presented to the International Labour Process conference 1 April 1993. In Halsey, A., Lauder, H., Brown, P. and Wells, A. (eds) *Education: Culture economy society*. Oxford: Oxford University Press.

Smyth, J. (1995) *Critical Discourses on Teacher Development*. London: Cassell.

Stenhouse, L. (1975) *An Introduction to Curriculum Research and Development*. London: Heinemann Educational.

Strathern, M. (2000) *Audit Cultures*. Abingdon: Routledge.

Stronach, I., Corbin, B., McNamara, O., Stark, S. and Warne, T. (2002) Towards an uncertain politics of professionalism: Teacher and nurse identities in flux. *Journal of Educational policy*, 17 (1): 109–38.

Training and Development Agency (2005). *Continuing Professional Development: National Priorities for Teachers*. Circular Annex B. Available at **www.tda.org.uk**

TDA (2008) *Continuing Professional Development Guidance*. London: TDA.

Wenger, E. (1998) *Communities of Practice*. Cambridge: Cambridge University Press.

Wenger, E. and Lave, J. (1991) *Situated Learning*. Cambridge: Cambridge University Press.

Whitty, G. (1997) Marketization, the state and the re-formation of the teaching profession, in Halsey, A., Lauder, H., Brown, P. and Wells, A. (eds) *Education: Culture economy society*. Oxford: Oxford University Press.

Young, M. (1998) *The Curriculum of the Future*. Abingdon: FalmerPress.

Index

Added to a page number 'f' denotes a figure and 't' denotes a table.